THE LAST KAMIKAZE

Vice Admiral Matome Ugaki, Imperial Japanese Navy.
Courtesy Masataka Chihaya.

THE LAST KAMIKAZE

THE STORY OF ADMIRAL MATOME UGAKI

EDWIN P. HOYT

PRAEGER

Westport, Connecticut
London

Library of Congress Cataloging-in-Publication Data

Hoyt, Edwin Palmer.
    The last kamikaze : the story of admiral Matome Ugaki / Edwin P.
Hoyt.
        p.   cm.
    Includes bibliographical references and index.
    ISBN 0-275-94067-5 (alk. paper)
    1. Ugaki, Matome, 1890-1945. 2. World War, 1939-1945—Naval
operations, Japanese. 3. World War, 1939-1945—Aerial operations,
Japanese. 4. Admirals—Japan—Biography. 5. Japan. Kaigun—
Biography. I. Title.
D777.U355H69   1993
940.54'4952'092—dc20
[B]   92-15694

British Library Cataloguing in Publication Data is available.

Library of Congress Catalog Card Number: 92-15694
ISBN: 0-275-94067-5

First published in 1993

Praeger Publishers, 88 Post Road West, Westport, CT 06881
An imprint of Greenwood Publishing Group, Inc.

Printed in the United States of America

The paper used in this book complies with the
Permanent Paper Standard issued by the National
Information Standards Organization (Z39.48-1984).

10 9 8 7 6 5 4 3 2 1

Copyright Acknowledgment

The author and publisher thank Masataka Chihaya for granting permission to use
the diary of Admiral Matome Ugaki and the photographs that appear in this book.

Contents

Photographs follow page 108.

Preface

This is the story of a man and a navy that shared a death wish—Vice Admiral Matome Ugaki and the Imperial Japanese Navy. In the end, which came in 1945, both achieved their wish, with enormous cost to the people of Japan. The Imperial Navy was physically destroyed and its slender remnants disbanded at the demand of the victorious Allies. Admiral Ugaki achieved the death wish he had held since 1941 by killing himself in what he knew was a totally fruitless cause, and against the will of his beloved Emperor Hirohito. After the Emperor announced the Japanese surrender on August 15 and called on all his subjects to "bear the unbearable" and pull together to build a new Japan, Ugaki stripped off his insignia of rank, climbed into a torpedo bomber, and flew to Okinawa, where his intention was to crash into an American ship. In fact, his aircraft and several others filled with ardent young men who had accompanied Ugaki on his last mission were all shot down by American nightfighters without achieving anything at all. Thus they joined the thousands of others, from Admiral Isoroku Yamamoto to the rawest farm boy, who had given their lives in Japan's fruitless drive for conquest.

The two tragedies, that of the navy and that of the man, are linked inseparably. They date back to 1937, the year the

Imperial Japanese Army forced Japan into the China Incident, which was to be the conquest and subjugation of Nationalist China and its enlistment in the Japanese cause of Asia for the Asiatics. Many Japanese naval officers opposed this adventure, including Admiral Yamamoto. There he parted company with Admiral Ugaki, who favored the subjugation of China and worked to further it as a plans and operations officer with the Imperial General Staff in Tokyo. At the outset of the China Incident Ugaki had his doubts, but they were soon swept away in a frenzy of jingoistic fervor. From that point on, as a highly placed navy official, he voted time and again for action that drove Japan inexorably toward war with the western powers. In 1940, at an Imperial Conference as a representative of the navy, he spoke up for the occupation of northern Indochina. This was seen as a necessary step to further the Japanese aims in China and beyond, for the movement into Indochina (when the French were on their knees after defeat by Germany) was a precursor to the invasion of Malaya and the Dutch East Indies, and everyone in army and navy circles knew it. Admiral Yamamoto opposed the move. Admiral Ugaki, who would later be his chief of staff of the Combined Fleet, favored it. Thus was indicated the deep split in the Japanese naval establishment.

By that time, 1940, the "Fleet faction" of the navy, to which Ugaki adhered, had triumphed over the "Treaty faction," to which Yamamoto belonged. Virtually all of the younger officers of the navy favored the Fleet faction; in fact, they constituted such a threat on the life of Admiral Yamamoto that his friend Navy Admiral Mitsumasa Yonai conspired to have Yamamoto removed as his deputy and sent to sea in command of the Combined Fleet to get him out of Tokyo and save his life.

It was then that the paths of Yamamoto and Ugaki crossed, for Ugaki was chosen by seniority and skill to be Yamamoto's chief of staff, although he was not Yamamoto's choice.

Although Admiral Ugaki had favored the aggressiveness of

the Fleet faction of the navy, he soon became aware of Admiral Yamamoto's views. Yamamoto had always held, along with Admiral Yonai and others who were versed in international affairs, that Japan had to live peaceably with the western powers. To go to war with them would be suicidal, because all one had to do was look at the statistics of natural resources. The British Empire and the United States abounded with all the fruits of nature: coal, iron, aluminum, and above all, oil, the blood of modern twentieth-century navies. Japan had virtually none of these. Therefore it was suicidal for Japan to even consider going to war with the western powers. It would be a war she could not win.

Admiral Yamamoto had also foreseen the effect the decision to invade Indochina would have on the United States. It would precipitate strong action. It certainly did. At that point the United States shut off all oil and steel exports to Japan. The United States was Japan's only supplier, so the Imperial Navy faced a future without oil. The Japanese militarists decided that if they could not have the oil by trading for it they would get it by conquest.

Associating with Yamamoto, Admiral Ugaki was very soon aware of and regretful about what he had done in favoring this course.

In 1940 and 1941 Admiral Yamamoto opposed the drift toward war as firmly as he dared, but he was fighting a rising tide. Admiral Ugaki was on the other side. Yet in the summer of 1941 both men attended a special meeting called by the navy minister of the senior admirals of the Imperial Navy. There the policy of the government, calling for war with the west, was revealed to them and they were asked to approve it. Admiral Yamamoto was the only one brave enough to rise and ask a question: Where was the Imperial Navy going to get the resources to carry on a war with the United States?

When that question was not answered, Yamamoto subsided. He could see that the way of the Japanese government was set. His battle was lost; Japan was going to war. His only options were to support the war effort and remain in the navy, or to resign his commission. As a loyal Japanese he chose to remain and fight, hoping that he could influence the course of history a little bit. After this meeting, Yamamoto turned his energies toward achieving success in an effort in which he had no confidence, to win a victory against the United States.

That meeting of admirals had another effect on Admiral Ugaki. For the first time he began to see Admiral Yamamoto's point that Japan did not have the resources to wage war against the west. Japan could not possibly win a war. She might win a quick victory and then perhaps persuade the Allies at the conference table to accept her own version of a Japanese destiny. That was the single hope, and by Admiral Yamamoto's own belief it was a tenuous one.

As he planned for the Pearl Harbor attack, which was in one blow to remove temporarily the striking power of the American fleet, Admiral Yamamoto lamented the need for and questioned the wisdom of what he was doing. Admiral Ugaki came to agree; as he refined and implemented Admiral Yamamoto's plans, he began to accept Yamamoto's assessment. It was then that Admiral Ugaki expressed his death wish. He would not survive the war, he decided. He would go down fighting in the service of his Emperor.

Introduction

Matome Ugaki was born in Okayama, a small city on western Honshu Island, and his first ambition was to go into the army and become a general.[1] But he joined the navy instead, and after graduation from Eta Jima naval academy he began the long slow climb through the officers' ranks to a point of distinction. In 1937 he was vice admiral and was appointed to the Naval General Staff as a section chief; as such he was an important person in the making of naval policy.[2] This was a time of great tension in Tokyo and within the navy. The China Incident began in July of that year and quickly blossomed into a full-scale war. The Rape of Nanking occurred at the end of the year, just after the *Panay* Incident, which involved the sinking of an American gunboat on the Yangtze River by Japanese naval carrier bombers and attacks by army artillery on several British gunboats.[3] As a member of the general staff, Admiral Ugaki was active in the formulation of policy in all these matters.

Although in the Japanese system the actual policies were made by consensus between the general staff and the minister of the navy, because Ugaki was a senior staff officer his views were always heard.[4] In 1940 he was present at several meetings of the Liaison Conference, which had taken the place of the Imperial Conference as the decisive meeting between the prime minister and his cabinet and the operating military leaders. Twice he stated his views in opposition to the Tripartite Alliance with Germany and Italy, and once, at an Imperial Conference, he stated his views in favor of the occupation of southern Indochina—which the Japanese undertook that year, causing the United States to cut off the flow of oil to Japan and stop all other trade with Japan.[5] One could say, then, that he was a typical naval officer, his eye was always on what he considered to be best for Japan and the navy. His position on the occupation of Indochina was based on the need to secure natural resources that many Japanese felt were being denied them by the big powers, the United States and Great Britain.

In the years before the war, Ugaki was a conservative member of the Japanese naval establishment. He was closer to the Fleet faction of the navy, which wanted expansion, than to the Treaty faction, which was willing to live with the limitation of having only three-fifths of the naval strength of Britain and the United States. When the China Incident began in 1937, he was not particularly concerned. Only as the months went on and there was no end to it did Ugaki begin to realize that the army had led Japan into a morass. He was distressed by this, as he said in the summer of 1941:

Four years have passed since the Chinese Incident occurred, but there is a long way to go before we shall be able to obtain our object. . . . Had the persons who were responsible for starting the Incident ever dreamed or realized that it would eventually develop into the present state? We cannot be proud of human wisdom.[6]

That statement was indicative of an aspect of Admiral Ugaki's character: He was of a philosophical turn of mind, much more so than the man he was serving as chief of staff, Admiral Isoroku Yamamoto. This philosophical bent led Ugaki to write a considerable amount of poetry during the war years, expressing his deep feelings about the conflict and the ways of humanity, and ultimately it led him to abandon his deepest personal loyalty to the Emperor in favor of what he considered to be a greater obligation to the young men he commanded in the last months of the war, hundreds of whom he had sent to their deaths as suicide pilots. Admiral Ugaki had not favored the establishment of the suicide campaign, yet he did not flinch when he was asked to take over its management and the ultimate air battle for the Japanese homeland. He undertook direction of the kamikaze corps as another naval duty, but with a difference: This time he promised the spirits of the young men he was sending to death that he would ultimately join them, and he did. Against the express orders of his Emperor, he set out on the final day of the war, after the surrender broadcast had ended everything for the Japanese, and he took his aircraft and several young men who insisted on going with him to their deaths off the shores of Okinawa.[7]

As a military gesture this was futile, and he knew it would be, but to him it was the symbol of his fulfillment of the deepest responsibility.

Much earlier in the war, Admiral Ugaki had laid modest claim to trying to resolve the problems attendant to the war in China as chief of the First Section of the Naval General Staff, but he had to admit that he had been unsuccessful. Four years after the start of the China war, he stood back and assessed his own part in it all. He had been one of the naval officers who had given consent, while knowing it was wrong, to Japan's entry into the Tripartite Alliance with Germany and Italy. Twice during the long interservice debate on the alliance he had stood against Japan's entry in liaison meetings between high government and high military officials, although to do so was actually dangerous because the Ministry of the Navy and the director of the Bureau of Military Affairs of the navy approved the plan. Ultimately he allowed himself to be dragooned into accepting the alliance, but he never felt comfortable about it. Now in 1941, as chief of staff to

Admiral Yamamoto, the commander of the Combined Fleet, Admiral Ugaki found himself in the position of planning the attack on the U.S. Pacific Fleet at Pearl Harbor, and he was not entirely happy about it. In this his views were certainly shared by Admiral Yamamoto. But both men were loyal Japanese navy officers, and their job was to fight wars, not to plan them. Previously, having held positions of power within the naval establishment, both men had in their own ways opposed the events that led them to this crisis. Knowing that the American reaction would be negative and strong, Ugaki had sensed that Japan's entry into the Rome-Berlin axis would bring disaster. But when he was approached by his own kind he had reluctantly assented, as had virtually every other admiral—including Yamamoto.

Having embarked on this course of action, the Naval General Staff did not even wait until the treaty was signed before starting to plan the war against the United States that they were sure would follow. Ugaki reproached himself for this move. He also reproached himself for failing to achieve a rapprochement with the Soviet Union, something he favored for Japan. He did not particularly like the Russians or their political system, but like many naval officers he felt encircled by the United States, Britain, the Netherlands, and China. He included China even though the Japanese seemed to be winning the war there. To him, the appearance of victory was quite deceptive; China was a trap into which the army had walked and now for reasons of face could not escape.

He worked manfully to achieve Russian rapprochement in 1940 and 1941, but the cards were stacked against him. Too many leading army officers belonged to the "Strike North" faction of the military clique, including General Tojo, who was war minister and ultimately became prime minister. The move ended in the resignation of the cabinet of Baron Hiranuma and thus ushered in the Konoye period, which was a last-ditch effort by the Emperor to avoid total army control of the destiny of Japan. The Hiranuma cabinet collapsed in what the Japanese called *fukuzatsu kaiki*, a situation both complicated and inscrutable.[8]

Admiral Ugaki also reproached himself later for advocating in an Imperial Conference, when Emperor Hirohito was present, the movement into southern Indochina in 1941, because it had played into the hands of the army. By the summer of 1941 when he began to keep a diary, Admiral Ugaki saw his country drifting rapidly and inexorably toward a war the navy did not want. He saw the Hull-Nomura conferences failing and the efforts of Prince Konoye to seek a face-to-face meeting with President Roosevelt come to naught because of Secretary Hull's intransigence. The navy men had been known to advocate the acceptance of most of the demands made by the United States on Japan, but they never had a chance because the American diplomats ignored the very important matter of face and offered the Japanese no way of getting off the hook on which they had impaled the nation in China.

Once the course to war was charted, Admiral Ugaki, like almost every other Japanese naval officer, made the best of the situation. It was, he said, the Combined Fleet's mission to assure the security of Japan and to defeat the outnumbering enemy through preparedness and vision, with every officer and every man remaining faithful to the Emperor. Thus, in October 1941, with a strong sense of destiny and an admission of guilty responsibility for what the navy had done in joining the decision for war, Admiral Ugaki took up his pen to keep the diary he called "Seaweed of War." He promised to bare his inner soul and the workings of his naval mind, for he knew that future historians would probe the events that were about to begin so fatefully in the next few months.[9] Already he had a sense of participating in the end of an era.

Admiral Ugaki was, by definition, the last kamikaze, but he was much more than that. He held many important positions in the Japanese navy, starting in the early days of the China Incident when he was a policy-making staff officer on the Imperial Naval General Staff. He then went to a sea command of a squadron of ships, only to be snatched from that assignment to take on the job of chief of staff of the Combined Fleet. He was traveling with Admiral Yamamoto in a separate plane (a precaution on which Yamamoto always insisted) when the Americans ambushed them in the Bougainville area in April 1943. Both twin-engined bombers were shot down; Ugaki's fell into the sea and he survived, but Yamamoto's crashed in the jungle. After the death of Yamamoto and a period of recuperation from his own wounds, Admiral Ugaki was appointed commander of battleships. He served in that position until the battle of Leyte Gulf in which the battleship *Musashi* was shot out from under him. When he returned to Japan in the fall of 1944, the naval establishment was in chaos. The fleet had been destroyed and the kamikaze concept had taken control of the naval air force. Admiral Ugaki was chosen to direct the naval effort at air protection of Japan, and this included Okinawa. It was, he was informed, to be a defense oriented entirely around the kamikaze concept. He moved to southern Kyushu to control the effort better and remained there for the rest of his life, supervising the dispatch of one-way air attackers by the hundreds.[10]

Admiral Ugaki's career was symbolic of the fate of the Imperial Japanese Navy. He rose to influence in a navy that became the most powerful in the Pacific, and he participated in all the battles in which that power was steadily eroded. At the end, his final charge into the teeth of the enemy was symbolic of the fate of the navy in which he had served all his adult life.

THE LAST KAMIKAZE

Preparing for Pearl Harbor

One day in the summer of 1940 Admiral Koshiro Oikawa, the Japanese minister of the navy, called a conference of admirals in Tokyo. This was an unusual event, but the circumstances were unusual. For ten years the navy had been suffering from a basic factional dispute. The dispute had begun after Japan's acceptance of the Washington Naval Treaty of 1922 and all the subsequent international treaties that limited Japan's naval forces to three-fifths of those of the United States and Great Britain. The navy had split more or less down the middle. What became known as the Fleet faction demanded the rejection of that 5-5-3 limitation and the building of a Japanese navy on a par with the U.S. and British navies. The Treaty faction advocated the acceptance of the limitation.

The Fleet faction won a triumph in 1935 when Japan rejected the Naval Treaty of 1934 and embarked on a naval building program that in four years would make the Imperial Navy the strongest in the Pacific. Thereafter the Fleet faction tried to ride roughshod over the opposition, but it did not succeed. The conservatives managed to maintain control of naval policy until 1940. But in that year the Imperial Army virtually seized control of the mechanism of civil government. Admiral Mitsumasa Yonai, a staunch member of the Treaty faction, was then the minister of the navy, and his deputy was Admiral Isoroku Yamamoto, the Japanese architect who had labored on the Naval Treaty of 1934. They staved off many power plays by the Fleet faction but in 1940 were in such danger of assassination that Yonai contrived to have Admiral Yamamoto posted as chief of the Combined Fleet, a sea job that got him out of Tokyo, and Yonai himself prepared to retire.[1]

Once Yonai and Yamamoto were gone from power, the Fleet faction began to assume control. It did this in cooperation with the power-hungry generals of the Imperial Army who were bent on military adventure (they had been since the 1920s when they began scheming to seize Manchuria and then China).

At the beginning of the European war, the expansionists of Japan wanted to cast their lot with the Germans and the Italians, who were challenging the imperial powers of France, Britain, and the United States. This sympathy for the "have not" nations of Europe became a vital matter in Japanese politics when the Rome-Berlin partnership was established in the late 1930s. Yosuke Matsuoka, the Japanese foreign minister in the cabinet of Prime Minister Prince Fumimaro Konoye, contrived to draw a Rome-Berlin-Tokyo treaty. Known as the Tripartite Treaty, it was designed primarily to (1) intimidate the United States, (2) keep the United States out of the war in Europe, and (3) by presenting the United States with three enemies rather than one, prevent the United States from taking strong action to stop Japanese expansion in the Pacific.[2]

Within the navy, all the animosities between the Fleet and Treaty factions now crystallized around this one issue, the Tripartite Treaty. Most of the senior officers opposed it, just as most of the junior officers supported it. The factionalism threatened to split the navy as never before. Thus Navy Minister Oikawa called the meeting of admirals on that summer day.

Admiral Yamamoto came up from the flagship *Nagato*

armed with reference materials and prepared to make a strong argument against the treaty. Admiral Ugaki was with him, although as befitted a junior vice admiral he was careful to keep quiet. Almost immediately on arrival, Admiral Yamamoto saw that the cards were stacked against him. This was not a meeting of admirals to settle the matter by reasoned argument, as he quickly discovered when Admiral Oikawa said that if the treaty was not signed the Konoye cabinet would resign. This meeting, then, had been called for the purpose of presenting a naval consensus. The pressure was on to show acceptance of the treaty. Admiral Yamamoto offered one argument in the form of a question: Japan got 80 percent of the resources the navy needed from the United States; if the treaty was signed, where would Japan get these resources?

Admiral Oikawa ignored the question and Yamamoto sat down. He realized then that there was no use arguing. In the time-honored fashion of the Japanese, having offered his objection and having failed, he raised his hand along with all the others when Minister Oikawa put the question. They all agreed, chief of staff Ugaki included, to accept the signing of the Tripartite Treaty.[3]

After that fateful day, the navy no longer could stand in the way of the army's ambitions. By September the decision to take over southern Indochina had been made and the troops marched. That decision was supported by Admiral Ugaki at an Imperial Conference even though Admiral Yamamoto called it the definitive step that made the war unavoidable.[4]

The reaction of the western powers was swift and decisive. The United States cut off all shipments of oil and steel to Japan and virtually stopped trade altogether. The British reopened the Burma Road, which they had closed earlier on Japanese insistence. This road led to war, and everyone in the military establishment knew it. But there seemed to be nothing to be done to avert the catastrophe. Admiral Yamamoto then began to prepare his plan for a preemptive strike on the

U.S. Pacific Fleet, and although final approval of the attack was still lacking at navy headquarters, Admiral Ugaki and the staff of the Combined Fleet worked out the details.[5] The ultimate decision to go to war was delayed, and delayed again, on the insistence of the Emperor. On October 16 the Konoye cabinet resigned, a fact that Admiral Ugaki and Admiral Yamamoto learned from Radio Tokyo. It was not hard for them to conclude that the resignation had occurred because of the policy toward the United States. Admiral Ugaki at that point was resigned to the coming of war. He felt it was inevitable because of the U.S. insistence on Japan's retreat from China as a precondition to the resumption of normal relations. Ugaki, and most of the Japanese people, could not accept the demand that they abandon China, into which they had poured fifteen billion yen and for which they had suffered a hundred and fifty thousand casualties. An indication of his feelings and the temper of the Japanese nation came two days later when, in a special ceremony at the Yasukuni shrine in Tokyo, the spirits of fifteen thousand casualties of the China war were enshrined. The Emperor paid a personal visit to the shrine that day. How could Japan simply withdraw from China like a beaten dog? There were many in the navy who, like Admiral Ugaki, rued the day that the army had ever dragged Japan into the China war. But now it was done and if Japan was to be extricated, someone would have to provide a reasonable way out. This was one aspect of the international situation to which the people in charge in Washington had given no consideration. Ugaki's feelings on the subject were deep. He noted in his diary that he would be content to die in the national service if he could join those at Yasukuni.[6]

Being convinced that war was inevitable, Admiral Ugaki hoped that Prince Konoye, whom he characterized as an easygoing man, would purge the liberal elements from his cabinet and get on with the war. But he really did not think Konoye capable of doing it. So he waited eagerly for news of the new prime minister, because the navy had to know which way the country was going as it formed its plan of attack on Pearl Harbor. And the navy could not wait long for action now that oil supplies had been cut off by the United States. Ugaki's personal view was that the government should be turned over to the military entirely.[7]

The Combined Fleet that day was in the midst of its training program for the coming operations in the south, off Morozumioki, with only the six carriers and their attendant ships absent. They were undergoing a special training program for the attack on Pearl Harbor; the torpedo squadrons were working at the southern Kyushu port of Kagoshima, which bears an uncanny resemblance to Pearl Harbor. So immersed was the fleet in preparations for war that the Harvest Thanksgiving Day was almost forgotten. This important Japanese celebration was usually marked quite formally, even at sea, with the officers and men putting on their formal uniforms. But this day Admiral Yamamoto felt there was no time for niceties, so he ordered Ugaki to signal the fleet that the celebration would consist only of assembling on the ships in battle uniform and making obeisances to the eastern sky. Ugaki carried out his orders, although giving the gods such short shrift was contrary to his personal beliefs.[8]

On the night of October 16 Radio Tokyo aired the big news: General Hideki Tojo had been selected by the Emperor to form the new cabinet. Admiral Ugaki was of two minds about this move. He knew that Tojo was a strong member of the war party in the army, but now what was left but the war party? All the generals who had opposed war had been purged by retirement. He expected Admiral Oikawa to leave the cabinet now and Admiral Yamamoto to be put out to pasture at some sinecure like the command of the Yokosuka Naval Base. He expected that Admiral Soemu Toyoda would be the new commander.[9]

But Admiral Ugaki was wrong, not understanding the enor-

mous hold that Admiral Yamamoto had on the navy. Yamamoto was undoubtedly the most popular and highly regarded
of all the seagoing admirals, and he was also the most able.[10]

October 1941 was occupied by training for the Pearl
Harbor operation even though final approval had not been
given by the Naval General Staff. During this training
Admiral Ugaki developed a negative opinion of Admiral
Chuichi Nagumo, who would lead the actual Pearl Harbor
striking force. He formed this opinion without any persuasion from Yamamoto because the two men were not close.
Ugaki had been picked as chief of staff of the Combined Fleet
by the navy personnel department, not by Yamamoto. So his
negative view of Nagumo was quite his own and was based
on Nagumo's attitudes and actions. It went back to the early
days of the China war when Nagumo had been a member of
the Naval General Staff and had not had the courage to speak
out against the incident created by the army. Nagumo's attitudes were so negative that Ugaki went to Yamamoto to sug-
gest that Nagumo resign his post and let someone take the job
who believed in it. Yamamoto concurred, but he refused to
complain to Tokyo. Ugaki's objections to Nagumo included
the following observations: (1) he lost his temper with his
subordinates, (2) he was given to bluffing when he was
drunk, and (3) worst of all, it was already October and he
was neither physically nor mentally prepared for the coming
operation against Pearl Harbor.[11]

October was a month of hard work accompanied by the
hard play for which the naval officers were famous. Yamamoto did not drink—it made him physically ill—but Admiral
Ugaki made up for him. Sometimes the admiral did not get to
bed until 3 or 4 o'clock in the morning during shore excur-
sions, as at Murozumi on October 16 when the staff spent the
night at a seashore hotel drinking and eating until the small
hours. Next morning bright and early Ugaki went fishing for
red snapper in a small boat, but the catch was so poor that he
quit at noon.[12]

Training continued with only a few interruptions. Admiral Yamamoto made a trip to Sasebo as part of an investigation of the sinking of an I Boat in the training exercises. Ugaki and the staff were very impressed by the admiral's devotion to duty, and he observed in his diary that with men like Yamamoto at the helm it would be easy to die for such a leader. Admiral Yamamoto returned from the trip to Sasebo much refreshed, which Ugaki noted in his diary. What he did not know was that Yamamoto had spent two days with his favorite geisha, who had become his lover and had replaced his wife in his affections. This was the first time he had seen her in months. Since he had left Tokyo to go to sea so had she, and she had opened a geisha house and restaurant on the side of a hill in Sasebo.[13] It was also the last time they would meet.

On November 1, 1941, Admiral Yamamoto received a message from Admiral Shigetaro Shimada, the new minister of the navy in the Tojo cabinet. Yamamoto was ordered to come to Tokyo in secrecy to call on the minister at his residence. Yamamoto brought the message to Ugaki and the two men conferred. What did it mean? Neither officer knew, but they understood that the demand for secrecy meant that it was something important. It might be the decision as to when they were to undertake the Pearl Harbor operation. Recently, because of the delays, Yamamoto had felt it might be put off until the middle of 1942. Ugaki recommended the date of December 8, 1941, on the basis of (1) it being a Sunday, when it was known the U.S. fleet was likely to be in port and not as alert as usual, and (2) the state of the moon on that day, which was most favorable. The worst thing he could imagine at this point was that the entire venture might be put off until the summer of 1942; to his mind that would be fatal.[14]

Yamamoto left the ship on the morning of November 2. He traveled by seaplane to Kure, where he caught a train for Tokyo. Admiral Ugaki settled down nervously to wait. November 3 was the anniversary of the birth of the Emperor Meiji, and Ugaki, being of a philosophical turn of mind, reflected on the great achievements of the Meiji era and the re-

sponsibility of the children of Showa to continue the great
works of the past and to assure the security of the Japanese
Empire. "When I consider the great achievements of the past
heroes and the sacred virtue of the Emperor [Meiji] with his
great glorious works, they inspire me with fresh courage."
His mind turned to duty and he composed a poem, which he
wrote into his diary:

> Minna shine.
> Minna shine,
> Kuni no tame
> Ore mo shinu.
>
> (Everyone dies.
> Everyone dies,
> For the sake of the nation
> I will die as well.)[15]

That night of November 3, Admiral Ugaki received a message from Yamamoto saying that he had cut short his trip and
would return to the flagship by way of Kure, arriving at Kure
on the afternoon of November 4. Ugaki knew then that the
decision had been made and that it must be what Yamamoto
wanted, because before the admiral left he had told Ugaki
that if the high command refused to go along with the Pearl
Harbor plan he would resign.

And then what?

He might go to Monte Carlo and become a gambler, Yamamoto had joked. That was something that had always
appealed to him, the gambler's life.[16]

As Ugaki waited for Yamamoto's return, he contemplated
events as reported in Tokyo and considered the policy that,
in his estimation, the government should be following. What
Tokyo should be doing just now was making warlike noises
for the benefit of the Americans. Then, if the noises drew a
belligerent response, Tokyo could pretend to back down. All
this was to mask the intention of the Japanese military
machine to begin and carry out the war.[17]

When Yamamoto returned to the ship on November 4, he had much to report. After the Tojo cabinet had been installed in mid-October, the Emperor had demanded a rethinking of the policy toward the United States and the difficulties the two countries were having. Tojo had complied and a dozen meetings had been held to discuss the situation. On November 4 it had finally been decided. The government would pursue a two-pronged policy: Continue to negotiate with the Americans, hoping for a breakthrough in the impasse that had developed, and at the same time prepare for war. The final decision would be made on December 1. As Yamamoto wanted, if it was to be war, I Day, or the day of the attack on Pearl Harbor, would be December 8.

Yamamoto also reported that he had been given an opportunity to get rid of Admiral Nagumo as head of the striking force against Pearl Harbor. Navy Minister Shimada, who had obviously heard at least some of the rumors about Yamamoto's dissatisfaction with Nagumo, had brought the matter up obliquely. Did the commander in chief want any personnel changes in the Combined Fleet on the eve of war? he had asked.

No, said Yamamoto. This was not the time for such change. The effect on the morale of the Combined Fleet would be too negative.[18]

Yamamoto still clung to a ray of hope that the war could be avoided. He had talked with Foreign Minister Togo, who wanted to propose some new initiatives. One would be a retreat from Indochina, to take affairs back to the point where they had been before the United States imposed the oil embargo on Japan. Then they could discuss the question of retreat from China.

Could one go back? Privately Ugaki doubted it, but he confined those thoughts to his diary.[19]

On November 6, Yamamoto and Ugaki went to Tokyo to put the final touches on Imperial Japanese Naval Order No. 1:

The Japanese Empire expects the opening of war against the United

States, England, and Holland at the beginning of December for the
sake of Japan's self-existence and self-defense and has decided to
prepare for the operations in every way.

Then followed the details. The Combined Fleet would keep
careful watch in the meantime to guard against surprise
attack from the United States. Mines would be laid in the
southern area, preparing for the day of attack on Malaya. In
the areas where there would be navy and army operations,
the operations would be carried out in accordance with an
army-navy agreement that had been hashed out by the admirals and generals a few weeks earlier. After the business
was completed in the next two days, a champagne party was
held at the minister's residence. Then Admiral Ugaki, who
lived in Tokyo, went home to his family. All were well but
complaining about the rationing and the shortage of con-
sumer goods that had already hit Japan. He listened but did
not pay much attention. None of them had lost any weight,
he noted.[20]

On November 10, at the Military Staff College in Tokyo,
the joint operating agreements between navy and army were
signed by Admiral Yamamoto and General Hiseichi Terauchi, who was then serving as commander in chief of the
armies that would invade Malaya and the south. At their
sides sat General Hajime Sugiyama, the army chief of staff,
and Admiral Osumi Nagano, the naval chief of staff.

All the command preliminaries were finished by November
10. Admiral Yamamoto, Admiral Ugaki, and all the navy
settled down to wait.

Preparing the Attack on Pearl Harbor

On November 13, 1941, one might say, the emotional preparations for the Pacific War began. Admiral Yamamoto and Admiral Ugaki went to the Iwakuni air base for a meeting of all the commanders of the fleets that would range far and wide around the Pacific, down to Malaya, to the Philippines, and to Hawaii. Admiral Yamamoto made an inspirational speech to these senior officers, and the details of the combined military and naval operations to start the war were explained to them. The admirals and captains then had their picture taken in a group, and they all autographed a sheet of paper that would be printed out and fixed to the prints.

"Nothing will be nicer memorials than these," observed Admiral Ugaki. The festive air was preserved that evening at a geisha party at the Fukagawa restaurant where the sake flowed copiously. The next day General Homma, who would lead the invasion of the Philippines, and several other general officers showed up to discuss army-navy cooperation in the starting of the war. That night there was another banquet, at which the admirals celebrated with the generals "our sure success in war." The next day a succession of generals and admirals arrived for consultation with Yamamoto, including General Terauchi, who would command the southern forces, and the vice chief of the Naval General Staff. Meanwhile

Yamamoto pondered the last chance for peace. Ambassador Kurusu arrived in Washington to reinforce Admiral Nomura in talks with the Americans in what Yamamoto suspected was a ploy and not a serious attempt to find common ground with the Americans.[1]

The flagship *Nagato* then took Admiral Yamamoto to Saeki, where the carrier *Akagi* was berthed, and on the afternoon of November 17 Admiral Yamamoto boarded the ship to make another inspirational address, this time to the airmen on their flight deck. Admiral Ugaki went along and was impressed with the faces of the young men as they listened to their commander in chief. "I saw on their faces unshakeable loyalty with determined resolution showing a sort of terribleness." That night the *Akagi* sailed for Hitokappa Bay on Etorofu Island in the Kuriles. It would not return to Japan until the Hawaii adventure either succeeded or failed.[2]

The ships kept going out and the senior officers of the fleets and squadrons stopped by the flagship to pay their respects. On November 19 Admiral Ugaki saw five submarines with midget submarines on their decks, the special submarine attack group destined for Pearl Harbor. He admired the young men's determined spirit—*kesshitai no seishin*—for these young men did not expect to come back.[3]

On November 25 Admiral Yamamoto issued an order to the striking force that would advance on Hawaii to destroy the American fleet at the outset of the war. The exact date of the attack would be given later, and the fleet was warned that if diplomatic negotiations succeeded, the task force would immediately be withdrawn without carrying out the attacks. At 6 o'clock on the evening of November 26, the Nagumo force left Hitokappa Bay in dense fog. Six carriers, two battleships, two heavy cruisers, one light cruiser, eleven destroyers, three submarines, and eight tankers sailed. Twenty-seven submarines from the Japanese Sixth Fleet were already converging on the Hawaiian area from several directions.

On December 1 Admiral Yamamoto left the fleet for

Tokyo to appear at the Imperial Palace for an audience with the Emperor and to accept the Imperial Rescript authorizing the attack on Pearl Harbor. He took with him a prepared speech of acceptance of responsibility on behalf of the Combined Fleet, which had been written for him that day by Admiral Ugaki.

Your humble subject is filled with trepidation and inspiration to have received Your Gracious Precept prior to the opening of war. Officers and sailors of the Combined Fleet will reverently swear to do their duty, all as one, and gain the objects of the war.[4]

That night Admiral Ugaki received a confidential telegram from the vice chief of the Naval General Staff ordering the opening of a top secret message that had been sent several days ago. When Ugaki opened it he found the orders to open hostilities against the United States, Britain, and Holland in the first ten days of December. Ugaki sent a message to Admiral Nagumo, who was at sea and approaching the international date line, saying that all had been decided but that the date would be ordered later.

On the morning of December 2 Admiral Ugaki ordered the staff to draft a message for Admiral Yamamoto to send to the fleet when hostilities were opened. It was to be in the tradition of Admiral Togo's message to the fleet at the battle of Tsushima Strait against the Russian Baltic Fleet:

The fate of our Empire depends on this fight.
Every man is expected to make the utmost effort.

Admiral Ugaki arrived at this message:

The fate of our Empire hangs upon this war.
Do your very best and even more than that.[5]

When he was finished, Ugaki was pleased with the result, which he thought compared favorably with Togo's message.

This was a busy day for Admiral Ugaki because the affairs of the fleet must proceed smoothly, no matter where Admiral Yamamoto might be, and Ugaki's responsibility was to be sure that everything worked as it should. At half past five that day he sent the message to the Nagumo force that everyone was waiting for: "Climb Mount Niitaka." This message was followed by one announcing that hostilities could begin as of one minute after midnight on December 8, Tokyo time.

It meant that the date of the attack was to be on the morning of December 8, with the proviso still in force that the commander in chief might call them back at the last minute because of diplomatic success. But the way the negotiations were going (and Admiral Ugaki followed the negotiations as carefully as he could from dispatches from the Naval General Staff), it did not seem likely that they would be crowned with success. The Americans showed no signs of yielding on the essential issue: the Japanese demand that there be no interference with their China operations. The Combined Fleet staff began to suffer from a bad case of the jitters. First came a message from an army air force source reporting seven unidentified ships at sea; then came a message that an army plane carrying copies of the general war plan was missing on a flight over China, and Admiral Ugaki had unpleasant visions of the plane being down and the Chinese reading the messages.

Admiral Ugaki whiled away the time, writing postcards to relatives and friends with an enigmatic poem he had composed:

> The time has arrived to take spirited action
> I swear we will do our very best for the nation and His
>   Majesty.[6]

These cards were then put aside for mailing in the navy post office just after the outbreak of war. When they arrived, the news of Pearl Harbor would have broken and the recipients would know what the cards meant.

On December 6, still saturated in the emotions of the hour, Admiral Ugaki wrote a letter to one of his sons, enclosing a bit of his hair and some clippings from his fingernails, usually symbols of impending death. To his second son he sent his admiral's flag, which had flown when he was commander of a cruiser squadron not so many months earlier. Admiral Ugaki was not going on the Pearl Harbor mission in body, but he certainly was going in spirit. And in several comments in his diary at about this time he referred to his own feeling that he would not live out the war.[7]

Aboard the flagship the tension grew hour upon hour. On December 6 it was reported that the Third Fleet in the south, which was descending on Malaya, had been shadowed by a British plane and that an order was sent to shoot it down. This was a worrisome matter because Admiral Yamamoto, and thus his staff, did not want any action taken before the strike on Pearl Harbor had become fact. There was talk about delaying the Malaya operation for a day, but Yamamoto vetoed the idea when it was offered by one of the staff. It would do more harm than good to make the change, he said, since everything had been arranged for the timetable at hand.

By December 6 the tension aboard the flagship was nearly unbearable. "Nothing more important than this will ever happen in the world," Ugaki wrote. "What a drama, risking the fate of the nation and so many lives."[8]

At 6 o'clock on the morning of December 7, Tokyo time, Ugaki sent off Admiral Yamamoto's message to the fleet, which Ugaki himself had so carefully composed. The attacking force was now deep in enemy water, and anything could happen. When the message was received the force was in the middle of fueling and preparing for the run into Pearl Harbor. The last tanker broke away and headed back to Japan that morning, and the Nagumo force increased speed to 24 knots and raced toward Pearl Harbor. On the carrier decks the planes stood wing to wing. The message was relayed to all the sailors of all the ships, and aboard the *Akagi* the Z flag, which was the selfsame flag that Admiral Togo had run up the mast of the flagship *Mikasa* at Tsushima, was now run up the carrier's mast.

The submarines were almost all in position around the Hawaiian islands. At noon on December 7 (Tokyo time) a message arrived from submarine *I-72*, which had been scouting Lahaina on Maui Island, reporting that the American fleet, which sometimes anchored off Maui Roads, was not anywhere in the area.

From Honolulu came the message that all the battleships were at their anchorages off Ford Island in Pearl Harbor but the staff was disappointed to learn that the carriers were nowhere in evidence. This fact gave rise to a debate within the staff of the Nagumo force. Should they delay the attack for a day or so, waiting for the carriers to arrive? Lieutenant Commander Kenjiro Ono, the intelligence officer, outlined the situation of the American carriers. The *Enterprise* had left Pearl Harbor on November 29, accompanied by two battleships, two heavy cruisers, and twelve destroyers. The battleships returned on December 6 but the other ships did not. The *Lexington* came into Pearl Harbor on November 29 but sailed on December 6 with five heavy cruisers. The *Saratoga*, he knew, was undergoing repairs at San Diego. And the *Wasp* was in the Atlantic Ocean. He thought the *Yorktown* and the *Hornet* must be somewhere in the area, and that the *Enterprise* should be returning to Pearl Harbor momentarily. So they could hope that some of the carriers at least might arrive before the attack the next morning. In any event, said Captain Tomatsu Oishi, the senior staff officer, they should be able to get all eight of the battleships. Commander Minoru Genda, an airman who had been responsible for the detailed planning of the air attack, observed that if two or three of the carriers were in harbor he would not care if all the battleships were out.

That was spoken like an airman, said Captain Oishi, but the facts were that the battleships were important game.

The debate continued, but it was settled by Rear Admiral Ryunosuke Kusaka, Nagumo's chief of staff, who thought there was only a slight chance that the carriers would come in on a Saturday or that the battleships would leave port over the weekend. He thought they ought to attack Pearl Harbor in the morning. And that was his recommendation, given to Admiral Nagumo that day and accepted on the evening of December 7, Tokyo time, December 6, Hawaii time.[9]

All day long on December 7 Admiral Yamamoto and Admiral Ugaki entertained visiting admirals who were preparing for various parts of the southern campaign. They seemed eager and willing to get to war in a hurry. As the responsible head of the fleet staff, Admiral Ugaki was keeping his eye out for trouble from many directions. He was particularly watching for action from the British battleship *Prince of Wales* and the battle cruiser *Repulse* and their attendant destroyers. They could throw a monkey wrench into the Japanese machinery, attacking the ships sailing for Thailand to attack Malaya. But although he monitored all the messages, there was nothing to worry about, he decided, because the British did not move to attack and the only excitement that afternoon was the news of the shooting down of a British seaplane off the Malayan coast that morning. The invasion fleet was moving steadily toward its destinations and had nearly reached them. So the success of the initial landings, at least, was now assured.

Assessing Japan's situation, Admiral Ugaki found reason for pride that day on the eve of the attack on the American fleet. Japan was as ready for war as a nation could be, he noted in his diary, "assiduous efforts" having been made to that end for two years. Of course it was an axiom of war that as one country prepared so did another, so that when Japan advanced a step so would the Americans. But considering the scarcities under which Japan suffered, he was quite proud of the extent of preparation.

The second reason for pride was that the navy had managed to awaken the army to the importance of the attack southward instead of the attack northward to the Soviet Union, which the army had already tried at Nomonhon.

The third reason was the Japanese adherence to the Tripartite Pact. At first it had seemed to be an error to pit Japan against the United States and Britain, but now, with the British on the defensive and the Germans and Italians winning in Africa and in Russia, the picture looked quite different. The war situation for the Axis was very favorable.

Fourth was the establishment of the Greater East Asia Co-Prosperity Sphere. To that end, British and American power in the Pacific must be destroyed and the Chiang Kai-Shek government as well, since China was in conspiracy with the anti-Axis powers.

Fifth was the results of the occupation of French Indochina. This action had produced much more powerful reactions from Britain and the United States than Japan had anticipated, resulting in the prohibition of exportation to Japan. But it was just as well that Japan had to face this problem squarely, instead of being bled to death.

Sixth was the choice of time to attack. This time, when the Americans, British, Chinese, and Dutch were surrounding Japan with the ABCD network, was high time to attack. If they had delayed as much as three years, the materials imbalance would have made an attack impossible to carry out.

Seventh, Japan was very lucky in her relationship with the Soviet Union. The army had missed its chance to take the initiative to fight the Russians, and it was just as well. Now it seemed unlikely that the Soviet Union would join the United States and Britain against Japan. The Russians had enough on their hands.

Eighth, they were lucky to have decided on this date in December. If they had delayed, the days would have added up to inaction.

Ninth, Japan was planning to come in like the typhoon, to get the necessary areas of control into Japanese hands and then to exploit them and protect them. Japan should then be able to continue the war for a very long time if necessary.

Tenth, Japan was lucky that the United States had behaved very foolishly in becoming so rigid in its attitudes. This was actually a good break for Japan because it forced agreement in the cabinet, where the civilians were holding out for peaceful means of settling the dispute, and the army was eager to go to war. The navy's attitude had changed from not wanting war to wanting war after the American position became so intransigent and the hopes for getting an oil supply from the United States seemed to be lost.

Eleventh, all these events had brought national policy to accord with the military strategy that must be pursued by Japan if the nation was to survive.

Twelfth, and finally, all this had come at just the right time. The strategic materials crisis had begun to develop two years before, and it had caused the military to prepare for a war that many Japanese did not want. The opportunity that lay before them now was their last, Ugaki was sure, because of the Allied policy of encirclement and strangling; if this opportunity had been missed it would have been very difficult for the navy to gear up again for action.[10]

Having noted all these thoughts in his diary on the eve of the greatest day he could remember, Admiral Ugaki closed his diary and went to bed.

The Attack on Pearl Harbor

At 5:30 on the morning of December 7, Hawaii time, the cruisers *Chikuma* and *Tone* launched two Zero float planes for a reconnaissance of Pearl Harbor. As they flew off, the last touches were being put on the carrier planes on the flight decks. The planes were lined up and the air crews were gathering in their briefing rooms. It was going to be a rough takeoff. The seas were high and spray was drenching the flight deck. Sometimes the handlers had to hold onto their planes to keep them from sliding along the deck and threatening to go into the sea.

Commander Mitsuo Fuchida, who would lead the air attack, entered the operations room and reported to Admiral Nagumo. He was already in his flying suit. Nagumo stood up and grasped the flier's hand. "I have confidence in you," the admiral said. Then he followed Fuchida into the briefing room where the captain of the *Akagi* was waiting with that ship's contingent of pilots. It was a small room, so small that not all the airmen could fit, and some had to stand in the passageway and listen to the briefing.

The carrier force was then 230 miles due north of Oahu Island. All the American ships in Pearl Harbor were identified on a blackboard. Commander Fuchida called the crowd to attention and turned to Captain Hasegawa for instructions.

"Take off according to plan," said the captain.

So the pilots and their air crews hurried out to the flight deck. The seas were running high, and the ship was pitching and rolling. Under training conditions this flight would have been delayed pending improvement in the weather conditions, but this was not a training mission. The decision was made to go. Commander Fuchida fastened a headband— *hachimaki*—around his head, a present from the maintenance crews, and got into his aircraft marked with red and yellow on the tail to identify him as commander of the air attack.

The *Akagi* turned to port and headed into the wind. The Japanese battle flag went up to join the Z flag. On the flight deck the green lamp was waving to signal: Time to go, and the first fighter started its engine. Then the fighter began to move, and it took off just before the ship started its downward pitch.

In fifteen minutes the first wave of 183 fighters, bombers, and torpedo planes was in the air from the 6 carriers and they were forming up in the dark sky, guided by signal lights of the lead planes. The air armada made one great circle over the fleet and set course for Oahu Island at 6:15 A.M.

Commander Fuchida's section consisted of forty-nine level bombers. Five hundred yards to the right were forty torpedo bombers; at about the same distance on the left and slightly above the level bombers were fifty-one dive bombers; flying overhead as cover were forty-three fighters.

They flew through thick cloud cover at 6,000 feet. The sun came through the clouds and they began to lighten. Commander Fuchida looked around him at the great formation of planes. They were traveling at 125 knots, and a little faster over the ground because of a tailwind. Fuchida tuned in to Radio Station KGMB, which had remained on the air all night long to home in some B-17 bombers that were flying to Hawaii from the mainland. He picked up the music, checked the direction by turning the antennae of his radio, and corrected the course of the Japanese armada. They had been 5 degrees off course.

The extent of American complacence was indicated by the fact that as he was wondering how the weather would be, the radio gave him a weather report. Partly cloudy it would be this morning, with clouds mostly over the Kohoolawe Mountain range. The cloud base would be at 3,500 feet, and the wind was north at 10 knots. He could not have asked for more information or more delightful information; he had worried that the Pearl Harbor base might be socked in with weather, and now he knew there would be holes in the cloud cover through which his men could attack.

Just after 7:30 A.M. the Japanese planes made their landfall on the northern shore of Oahu. They were over Kahuku Point, the northern tip of the island. Now Commander Fuchida had to decide what tactics he would use for the attack. If they had the surprise factor, the torpedo planes would strike first, then the level bombers, and then the dive bombers. But if resistance was expected, the dive bombers would go in first to cause confusion and attract enemy fire, the level bombers would follow, concentrating on anti-aircraft installations, and then the torpedo planes would attack the ships.

Commander Fuchida was waiting for news from the reconnaissance planes that had taken over from the *Chikuma* and the *Tone*. But there was no word. He decided that the surprise factor was still with them so he fired a single flare, the signal for attack.

In response the dive bombers rose to 12,000 feet, the torpedo bombers went down to treetop level, and the level bombers hovered just under the clouds. But the fighters did not react at all. Fuchida decided they must have missed the signal, so he fired another flare. The fighters noted and began speeding toward Oahu. But to the others this second flare meant a different signal. It signified that they had been discovered and that the attack would not be a surprise attack. That meant to the commander of the dive bombers that his group was to attack first of all.

The matter was compounded because some pilots had

understood the first signal and others had not. So the Japanese formation began to break up. Meanwhile the report came in from the reconnaissance planes, giving weather and cloud information and also the fact that there were no carriers in the harbor. But by this time Commander Fuchida could see the battleships, all lined up around Ford Island, eight of them. He ordered the attack: *Totsugeki*, or CHARGE! The code for the attack was *To* repeated over and over. His radio operation began tapping out *To To To To To To*. . . .[1]

Admiral Ugaki had slept soundly until 3 A.M. Tokyo time, when he awakened without anyone calling him. He got out of bed and lit a cigarette. A staff officer came into the room.

"The radio is picking up the transmission of *To To To*. . . ."

Admiral Ugaki hurried to the operations room, and the telegrams started coming in, messages picked up from the planes in the air over Oahu.

"I struck an enemy battleship with great results. . . ."

"I bombed Hickam Airfield. . . ."

He also looked over the messages picked up from the American radio. They showed the thorough confusion of the Americans.

"All ships in Pearl Harbor sail. . . ."

"Sweep the magnetic mines and moored mines in the waters south of Ford Island. . . ."

That message puzzled Admiral Ugaki until he reasoned that the midget submarines, which had penetrated the harbor, must have been mistaken by someone for magnetic mines.

"Commander in chief, Asiatic Fleet [Manila] will operate according to Plan No. 4. . . ."

"SOS attacked by Jap bombers. . . ."

"Ships' nationality unknown ten miles off point. . . ."

"Japs. . . . This is the real thing. . . ."[2]

The first attack was very successful and left the battleships sunk or burning. Hickam Field was hard hit, as was Wheeler Field to the northwest. It took the Japanese planes about an hour to complete their mission and they lost 3 fighters, 1 dive bomber, and 5 torpedo bombers. As they headed homeward the second attack force of 171 planes came in. This attack concentrated on Hickam Field and Kaneohe Naval Air Station except for the dive bombers, which again came in to hit the ships in Pearl Harbor. The second attack also lasted about an hour. Its losses were high: The Japanese lost 6 fighters and 14 dive bombers.[3]

Commander Fuchida waited until the last planes had attacked, and then he rounded up a pair of stray fighters and took them back to the carriers with him. His plane was the last to land on the *Akagi*, and he saw that rearmed and refueled planes were being lined up on the deck. As soon as the wheels of his plane stopped turning he was called to the bridge for an account of the attack. When he got there he could see from the faces that a heated discussion had been in progress and he knew it was about the next attack. They were waiting for his account of the battle.

He reported that four battleships had definitely been sunk. Admiral Nagumo said that meant they had carried out their mission and had secured the results that were wanted.

On the bridge then they discussed the extent of the damage on the airfields. When he was asked for his views, Commander Fuchida said, "All things considered we have achieved a great amount of destruction, but it would be unwise to assume that we have destroyed everything. There are still many targets remaining that should be hit. Therefore I recommend that another attack be launched."[4]

But Admiral Nagumo decided against another attack. He had been nervous about this mission from the outset and was afraid of the American carriers, whose whereabouts he did not know. So he decided to cut and run, although virtually all of his airmen wanted to stay and finish the job. The orders were given and the Japanese fleet moved off as swiftly as it had come, leaving a Pearl Harbor that was surprisingly undamaged although the battleships and a few other ships were sunk and most of the aircraft destroyed.

Aboard the flagship that day, Admiral Ugaki checked the messages carefully as they came in. He and Admiral Yamamoto were pleased with the results of the day. The first Japanese troops had landed on Bataan Island, a preliminary for the landings to come in Lingayen Gulf. The air force from Taiwan was attacking the Philippines and securing good results. The Japanese forces had landed successfully in Malaya. Thailand had gone along with Japan's proposal to let Japanese troops pass through and for the Japanese to use Thai military facilities. There had been some fighting by local units when the Japanese marched into Bangkok, but this was stopped by the Thai military authorities and the Japanese were welcomed. The army had begun to move against Hong Kong. On the Yangtze River several British and American gunboats had been captured or sunk.

Late in the day Admiral Yamamoto received a message from the Nagumo force. They said they had sunk two battleships and badly damaged four cruisers and shot down three hundred planes. They also claimed to have sunk one aircraft carrier, a claim that had to be negated very quickly. For all that, the Japanese fleet had lost about thirty aircraft.

"Generally speaking," Admiral Ugaki wrote in his diary, "this is a great success. First come first served."

On December 9, Tokyo time, the telegrams of congratulation began to come in from the Naval General Staff, the navy minister, the minister of war, and from General Terauchi.

And there was word from the United States: war against Japan was declared. Admiral Ugaki took special note of a message from Secretary of the Navy Frank Knox to all the ships at sea and all the American naval stations: "The first treacherous attack by the enemy navy has been a tremendous shock." There was no time to be lost, he said. The American people wanted as many ships and guns and people as they could get, the sooner the better.

"How crazy it is," was Admiral Ugaki's comment. "This meant the Americans had suffered an absolute knockout."[5]

All was going well except for one set of landings at Kotabaru in Malaya. There the Japanese were suffering some losses and the going was difficult. Another bit of news came to Admiral Ugaki that day. The submarine *I-65* had sighted two major enemy ships off the coast of Malaya. (These were the battleship *Prince of Wales* and the battle cruiser *Repulse*.) When this word came into the operations room of the fleet flagship, the staff jumped. A flood of orders was issued—to the submarine to shadow the ships, to the naval air stations in Indochina to be prepared to attack.

These ships had been identified earlier at Singapore by Japanese reconnaissance planes, and an attempt had been started to attack them after the Pearl Harbor attack opened the war. But the search plane that found the vessels had delayed an hour in reporting on them. Now that had been rectified by the rediscovery of the British ships off the Malay coast by the *I-65*. It was too late in the day to do anything, but the morrow would come, and with it an attack would be made.

As Admiral Ugaki considered the damage done at Pearl Harbor and the loss of only thirty planes, he wondered why Admiral Nagumo had not made at least one more attack. Several members of the staff suggested that Nagumo be ordered to return and attack Hawaii again. But Admiral Yamamoto would not force Nagumo to do so. To do this, he said (and Admiral Ugaki had to agree), would be to destroy the morale of Nagumo's force. Privately, Ugaki said that were he in Nagumo's shoes he would make every attempt to destroy the Pearl Harbor base completely.

But since the task force had already scuttled for home, there was nothing to be done, said Admiral Yamamoto. Admiral Ugaki then proposed that the task force be given an additional task, and Yamamoto agreed. The order was sent to Nagumo to attack Midway Island on the return voyage, if circumstances permitted. The latter phrase was put in at the insistence of Yamamoto, who refused to interfere with Nagumo's operations, although personally he was much angrier with Nagumo for not finishing the job than anyone knew. Instead of an unqualified success, which Imperial General Headquarters was crowing about, Yamamoto knew that the Pearl Harbor raid, because it left the job of wrecking the bases unfinished, had been only the most limited success.[6]

On the morning of December 10 Admiral Ugaki turned his attention to the British warships, the *Prince of Wales* and the *Repulse*, which were sailing in Malayan waters and looking for an opportunity to disrupt the Japanese landings. On the night of December 9 he learned from the message file that the enemy had turned south after running up toward Indochina and that the *I-65* had given chase and fired several torpedoes, but they all missed. They also avoided the Japanese minefields. So this morning Admiral Yamamoto decided that the attack would be carried out by his land-based naval air forces from airfields in Indochina. The two British ships were attacked by fifty-one torpedo bombers that day. The *Repulse* sank at 2:20 in the afternoon, and the *Prince of Wales*, which the Japanese at first misidentified as the *King George V*, sank half an hour later. The Japanese losses were three planes shot down. A handful were forced to make emergency landings due to damage, but they managed to make it to the Indochina shore.[7]

As for the British ships, Ugaki noted that the water where they sank was shallow—only about 50 meters deep—and that the navy expected to salvage the vessels and put them in the service of the Japanese navy. It was an ambitious plan, and one that would never be realized as the war turned around within the year.

As for the battle, Ugaki realized that it proved that "battleships are nothing and airplanes are everything" in modern war.

Admiral Ugaki and Admiral Yamamoto were gravely interested in the operations of the midget submarines at Pearl Harbor. Their employment had been a sort of experiment. By the third day after the attack it was apparent that all five of the midget submarines had been lost but that at least three of them had penetrated into Pearl Harbor, where they were mistaken at first for mines but were then identified and sunk without doing any damage. Admiral Ugaki pulled out a photograph and collection of autographs taken at the Navy Officers club at Kure in November when he attended the farewell party for these young men. Each had written his name and a slogan on a piece of paper that was passed around, and Ugaki had collected them—and the group photo—and framed them. Now he gazed at it as he pondered the deaths of these brave young men.

Lieutenant Naoji Iwasa had written "Loyalty and Patriotism."

Lieutenant Keiu Matsuo had written "Sincerity."

Lieutenant Masaharu Yokoyama had written "Even a demon will make way if I go against him."

Lieutenant Shigemi Fururo had written "Coolness and Decision."

Ensign Akira Hiroo had written "Patriotism through Eternity."

Ensign Kazuo Sakamaki had written "Prudence and Courage."[8]

Now they were all dead, along with the crewmen of each of the five small submarines, and Admiral Ugaki mourned them. (Actually, they were not all dead: Ensign Sakamaki had survived. His midget submarine, with its gyrocompass out of order, had washed up on the northern shore of Oahu. He had gotten out of it more dead than alive. He was captured on the beach and held in an American prison camp for the balance of the war.)

That day was the navy's day. An Imperial rescript arrived at the flagship from the Emperor praising the Combined Fleet on what he called its great success.

The Combined Fleet, at the beginning of the war, has gained a great deal of merit by destroying the enemy fleet and air strength at Hawaii through appropriate strategy and valiant fighting. We highly approve of this. We hope our subjects will strive for future victory with their best efforts.[9]

Admiral Yamamoto was pleased, of course, but he and Admiral Ugaki realized that this was only the beginning and that they must not succumb to overconfidence, as the Imperial General Headquarters was already doing.

It was hard not to feel exultation. The Imperial forces were on the move everywhere. That day the naval forces in the south occupied the British-mandated Gilbert Islands. And from Hawaii came word that indicated what a shock the Americans had been dealt by the Pearl Harbor attack. A news report indicated that the naval leaders involved, including Admiral Kimmel, were to blame. Admiral Ugaki observed that it was "gross error for the authorities to punish their subordinates when some misfortune occurs. When a state wants to press its national policies [as the United States had done against Japan], then that state must be prepared for war. The responsibility really rested with the President."[10]

Here was a case where the enemy saw the picture much more clearly, that President Roosevelt and Congress were looking for scapegoats and found them in Admiral Husband Kimmel and General Walter Short, the military commanders in Hawaii. It would not be until the end of the war that anyone dared question this destructive policy, and then Admiral King, the commander of the navy, would note that Kimmel and Short had been sacrificed uselessly and needlessly on the altar of an uninformed public opinion.

Victories

Following the navy's landings of the Imperial Army troops in Malaya, that campaign devolved to the army and Admiral Ugaki and the Combined Fleet were only peripherally concerned. But the navy had an enormous responsibility in the Philippines—to knock out the American air forces and naval forces and to destroy the naval bases in preparation for the army campaign there.

On December 11 the Combined Fleet flagship received bad news from the south. The Wake Island expedition had failed, and two destroyers had been sunk by the Americans. So the entire expedition was withdrawn to the Marshall Islands for regrouping, but the effort was not to be given up.

In compensation Admiral Ugaki had excellent news for Admiral Yamamoto about the Philippines. The Japanese air attacks on the Clark Field complex near Manila had destroyed more than half the planes of the American air forces. The airmen reported that they had shot down and destroyed 106 planes and that only about 50 remained. They did not expect much resistance from these. Ugaki was mildly annoyed by the communiqué from Imperial Headquarters that indicated that the army planes had been responsible for this destruction, because in fact the army planes were nowhere about. It was strictly a navy show.

That day Admiral Ugaki took time to consider the impli-
cations of political events of the last two days. Germany and
Italy had declared war on the United States, and on December 11 the United States had declared war on Germany and
Japan. "Now it really has turned into a second world war,"
Admiral Ugaki confided to his diary. "Everything rests on the
shoulders of our empire in so far as leadership of the new
world order is concerned. The Rome-Berlin-Tokyo axis will
become the center of the world."[1]

Admiral Ugaki, representing one segment of Japanese
naval thinking, fully expected war with the Soviet Union.
That was one reason he had advocated this strike against the
south in the winter. It would give Japan time to consolidate
its new gains and prepare for the possibility of the Russians
coming into the war against them after the spring thaws.

On December 12 the Japanese landed at Legaspi on southern Luzon Island. That was good news. But the news from
Wake Island was not so good. The Wake Island occupation
force had demanded another aircraft carrier for reinforcement. So the situation looked cloudy and not hopeful. The
fact was that the Wake occupation had been repelled; and at
one point three American carriers were approaching Wake
with reinforcements, which meant they had the ability to
destroy the Wake Island force. Admiral Ugaki did not know
it, but the timidity of the admiral who had replaced Admiral
Kimmel in temporary charge of the Pacific Fleet is all that
saved the Japanese occupation force from disaster. Admiral
Pye, the temporary commander, ended up calling back the
three carrier task forces that Admiral Kimmel had sent out to
make the relief and lure the Japanese into a fight.[2]

Since the Pearl Harbor attack, the flagship *Nagato* and the
major elements of the Combined Fleet had been at sea, hover-
ing between the Japanese islands and the Kerama Retto in
case they were needed either in the south or in the Philippine
area. During the night of December 11, Admiral Ugaki was
taking a bath when suddenly a submarine alert was sounded.

He hurried to dress and get to the bridge. A patrol plane dropped a depth bomb about 2 miles to the starboard side of the flagship. Two destroyers streamed out to make a depth charge attack. The *Nagato* radiomen claimed that they intercepted wireless messages between two submarines, in the clear. But there was no attack, and the destroyers did not make any claims to have sunk any submarines.

On December 12 the flagship received another Imperial rescript, this one congratulating the navy for destroying the *Repulse* and the *Prince of Wales*. Admiral Ugaki reverently quoted the rescript and Admiral Yamamoto's response in his diary: "Your humble subject is filled with trepidation with your rescript again. Reverent. Replying, Yamamoto."[3]

These interchanges, which would be repeated again and again as the war developed, were completely serious. They constituted a representation of the relationship of the navy and its officers and sailors with the Emperor, who was not only their commander in chief but a god figure to them. The Emperor was the personification of Japan and all that these men were fighting for, firm in their belief that they had been forced into this war by the intransigence of the Americans and the British. Admiral Yamamoto did not share this feeling, but now that war was a reality, he was determined to prosecute it as decisively as he could. He had in effect put the political processes behind him when he stepped out of the navy ministry and aboard the Combined Fleet flagship. He was now just a cog in the Japanese military machine, and his views of events more nearly coincided with those of Admiral Ugaki than they had before. Yet there was an enormous gap between the two men and between Admiral Yamamoto and the naval high command. Ugaki took at face value the actions of the high command and the claims made by Imperial General Headquarters; Yamamoto was too shrewd and too experienced to believe them. And he lamented the excessive claims that the naval spokesmen in Tokyo were already beginning to make about the victories that had been achieved.[4]

On December 13 the fleet passed through the Hayasui Channel and headed eastward, arriving that evening at the Hashirajima anchorage. By this time Admiral Nagumo's force should have carried out their instructions and attacked Midway Island on their way home. But there was report of an air attack. Ugaki went to bed that night wondering what had happened to Nagumo's force.

On December 15 Admiral Ugaki learned to his chagrin that Admiral Nagumo had not attacked Midway Island after all, pleading bad weather. On the flagship they did not believe the tale. Nagumo's force was now heading for the safety of Truk, still fearful of the American carrier forces they had never been able to find. Ugaki was quite disgusted with them and hoped that when they put in at Truk they would at least give a hand to the southern forces that were having so much difficulty with the Wake Island attack.[5]

But Nagumo again confused the issue. Perhaps fearful that he might be asked to undertake a new operation at Truk, he abruptly changed plans and headed for Japan. Ugaki conferred with Admiral Yamamoto and received permission to order Nagumo to make a strike on Wake Island, so he sent the orders. And that day there was new excitement at Hashirajima: The battleship *Yamato* appeared. This super-battleship with eighteen-inch guns was to be the pride of the Japanese fleet and soon to be the flagship of the Combined Fleet. She and her sister ship, the *Musashi*, were expected to play major roles in the war at sea.

Wake and the Philippines dominated life aboard the flagship. The news from Wake was fragmentary. On December 22, learning that the Japanese forces had landed safely in Lingayen Gulf and had met no enemy resistance, Ugaki had the feeling that things were going very well indeed. "I sense that the enemy has lost his fighting spirit." He predicted that the fall of Singapore would come much sooner than anyone expected. Hong Kong he expected to capitulate momentarily. He was right—three days later Hong Kong surrendered to overwhelming force.[6]

Ugaki and the staff were on pins and needles about Wake, which seemed to them to represent the greatest challenge the navy had yet faced. It came to an end on December 23. Once the American task forces were called back, the marines on Wake received no more aircraft with which to defend the island. They ran out of ammunition and were overwhelmed. But the Japanese performance had been so poor and so ragged that the commander of the Fourth Fleet, who was responsible for the Wake Island attack, was relieved of his command.[7]

The war came home personally to Admiral Ugaki that day. The fleet received a message that one of the naval aircraft taking part in the Legaspi attacks had crashed on takeoff and exploded and that the commander, Lieutenant Nishimura, had been one of those killed. The lieutenant was the son of Admiral Nishimura, commander of the Second Destroyer Squadron of the fleet, and an old acquaintance of Admiral Ugaki. When Ugaki was captain of the *Hyuga*, one of the two hermaphrodite battleship carriers of Japan's navy, Midshipman Nishimura had been one of the young naval cadets assigned to the *Hyuga* for sea training. Captain Ugaki had taught him navigation. His father, the admiral, had observed one day, "You taught him pretty well; I appreciate it." And once, when Ugaki was chief of the First Department of the Naval General Staff, young Nishimura had come to his house with two friends on a Sunday just to pay a social call. A picture was taken of them then, one that Ugaki still had of days fondly remembered. He could only hope that somehow Lieutenant Nishimura had been saved.[8]

Late on December 23 the Nagumo task force arrived in the bay and anchored. Admiral Ugaki went out to the flagship to pay a courtesy call, and he learned that Nagumo's staff had been annoyed by being ordered to attack Midway. They had not done it. Next morning, Nagumo's staff and the admiral came aboard the *Nagato*. Nagumo and the staff made reports, nothing was said about the way in which they had carried out their mission, and the discussions were followed by a drinking party that lasted until luncheon. Admiral Ugaki, who had a toothache, retired from all this early.

The year 1941 ended on a note of triumph. There were Imperial rescripts for the China army forces congratulating them on the capture of Hong Kong, and much excitement in Tokyo about the speed with which General Tomoyuki Yamashita was moving down the Malay Peninsula toward Singapore.

Admiral Ugaki greeted in the new year with mixed emotions. He hoped the war would end quickly, as of course it had to if it was to be a victory for Japan. Ugaki knew as well as anyone that the vast resources of the United States had not yet been tapped and that they definitely would be brought into play. He had mentioned this several times in his earlier diary entries. But now, along with most of Japan, he was filled with a sense of euphoria. "It has been only twenty-five days since the war started, yet the operations have been progressing smoothly and we have enough reason to hope for completion of the first stage of the war before the end of March. Then what will come next?"

He was concerned about the "rash and thoughtless acts of the army" that might drag Japan into war with the Soviet Union. He was also concerned that the Americans and the British might recover their strength enough to fight a decisive battle in the Pacific. But on balance he felt that the future was bright.[9]

On New Year's Day the submarine *I-3* reported the sighting of an enemy carrier task force 100 miles west of Oahu, heading west. Ugaki wondered what was intended. Was it merely a patrol, or was it an attack force heading out to hit some Japanese base? Obviously it was not powerful enough to be heading toward Japan, so that was no worry for him. But he and Yamamoto decided to try to lay a trap for the force, using submarines. A flotilla was made ready at Kwajalein in the Marshalls, and another flotilla on the return trip from the west coast of the United States could sweep in from the rear. Besides, bombers and flying boats could be sent from the new base at Wake Island.[10]

On January 2 the submarines at Kwajalein were sent out. But that was the end of it. The submarines searched and never caught the task force, and the Japanese patrol planes from Wake did not find them either. It was not difficult to know why. The Americans at this point were still strictly on the defensive and no carrier forces were venturing forth to attack the enemy. They moved back and forth between Hawaii and the mainland and ventured out to sea as far as Midway, but no attacks were in progress nor would they be for two months. Admiral Nimitz had just arrived at Pearl Harbor and was still dealing with logistical, personnel, and morale problems.[11]

Here one of the essential weaknesses of the Japanese naval strategy was revealed. When the submarines failed to make contact with the American carrier force, Admiral Yamamoto was quite disgusted. "In the Naval Conference [1934] Japan opposed the abolishment of the submarine on the grounds that they were defensive weapons and never offensive, and now it seems that they have become really defensive. However, if they can sink a warship their spirit will rise."[12] This was an indication of Japanese thinking about the submarines. At a time when the Germans and the Americans were conducting unrestricted submarine warfare against merchant shipping, with an eye to destroying the enemy's ability to make war, the Japanese were considering the submarine primarily as a weapon to sink other naval vessels. This was a primary reason for the ineffectiveness of Japan's submarines in relation to their strength.[13]

By the afternoon of January 2 it was apparent aboard the flagship that the Japanese Forty-eighth Division would capture Manila on the following day. The Philippine campaign seemed nearly over.

And the euphoria continued. On New Year's Day, a time of

major celebration in Japanese life, the newspaper published photographs of the Pearl Harbor attack to impress the Japanese public. "The people seemed to be delighted," wrote Admiral Ugaki in his diary.

On January 3 the Japanese did indeed enter Manila, which General MacArthur had declared to be an open city to save it from destruction. But aboard the flagship there was puzzlement. What had become of the garrison, and where had MacArthur and the other leaders gone? Admiral Ugaki hazarded a guess that they had fled to Australia or to Corregidor. He was right in the latter, although in the euphoria of the time he did not have any suspicion that the conquest of the rest of Luzon would be a long and difficult process—and that it might have been stopped had the American high command not decided to sacrifice the Philippines in order to concentrate on the prosecution of the war in Europe.[14]

Admiral Yamamoto and Admiral Ugaki were already planning what part the navy might play in the attack on Corregidor and the American-controlled access to Manila Bay. Their thinking at the moment was that it should be accomplished by an attack on Corregidor with 800-kilogram bombs and, after a sustained bombing program, an amphibious landing from the bay.[15]

On January 3 Admiral Ugaki and Admiral Yamamoto concerned themselves with learning the facts about the midget submarine operations at Pearl Harbor. The I-16, one of the submarines that had carried a midget submarine to Pearl Harbor, was called to Hashirajima for a report by its skipper to the admirals. He came on that day and made the report. Yamamoto and Ugaki listened carefully. They saw that there was much to be learned about the employment of midget submarines before they were used again in a fleet operation.

Already operations at sea as well as on land were far ahead of schedule. The Third Fleet was now going to be dispatched for operations in the Dutch East Indies, which had originally been scheduled for March.

It was apparent on this January day that the Americans had not lost their fighting spirit. To the flagship came the news that eight American B-17s had raided the Mararag anchorage near Davao and had put one bomb into the cruiser *Myoko*, the flagship of the Fifth Carrier Division. The bombs caused damage to three turrets, and there were sixty casualties. The flag was moved to the *Nachi* and the *Myoko* was sent to Takao, Taiwan, for repairs.[16]

On January 5 the carrier task force was sent out again, this time for operations in the Rabaul area, to support Japanese military operations there. Everything was going splendidly. Admiral Ugaki and Admiral Yamamoto expected to complete the first stage of naval operations by the middle of March. What then? Would they attack Australia, or India, or move against Hawaii? Would they go against the Russians in the north, as the army wanted to do? Admiral Yamamoto told Admiral Ugaki to start thinking about the alternatives so the fleet could present some plans to the naval high command. Those plans had to be established by the end of February. So Ugaki that day put his senior staff officers to studying the possibilities. The senior staff officer suggested that they keep the war in the south so that the army would not be tempted to attack the Soviet Union, which it so dearly wanted to do. Yamamoto concurred. He knew Prime Minister Tojo, and he knew that Tojo was a "Strike North" man who wanted to attack the Soviet Union.[17]

But already certain strategic factors were apparent. First, they must expect the recovery of the U.S. military strength, and quite soon. They also believed the British would be able to send more forces to the Far East. If the Russians faced defeat in the west by the Germans, then they would have to yield to American demands that Russian territory be used for the war against Japan.

But if the Germans succeeded in the Soviet Union, which now seemed more doubtful than before, it might be necessary to share a victory with the Germans, who would want the

Japanese to fight in India and westward. Japan should be careful to limit its operations to the areas in which it found the resources it needed; Japan should not expand farther. Matters such as an Indian attack might be possible if only a few war materials and people were needed. But Japan had to remember its limitations and keep a strong reserve of fighting strength.

And what about Hawaii? Tempting as it might be, an attack there could be accomplished only after a decisive battle eliminated the power of the Pacific Fleet, which Nagumo had failed to do in the Pearl Harbor attack.[18]

Admiral Ugaki also proposed to send submarines to raid the Panama Canal and Bombay, but Admiral Yamamoto had not approved such operations yet.

By January 7 Admiral Yamamoto was working on the invasion of Java, which had been advanced to February 26 because the operations in the south had been so successful.

On January 8, when the war was exactly one month old, Admiral Ugaki took the occasion to examine Japan's situation. He found it wanting. The problem was that in Tokyo there were no statesmen of quality. "However invincible the Imperial armed forces are, and however great their exploits may be, the great achievement done at sacrifice of our lives will be only in vain, unless statesmen have a great policy for the country."

He looked across the sea at the meetings between U.S. President Roosevelt and British Prime Minister Churchill and their establishment of a unified command for the Allied powers. His attitude was truculent, as befitted a victorious Japanese admiral, and he spoke of them "looking for places to hide," but it was apparent that he was concerned about Japan's lack of statesmanship in her counsels.[19]

Despite all the brave words, Admiral Yamamoto and Admiral Ugaki were very concerned about the enemy's ability to raid Tokyo. Ugaki mentioned the need to improve the air raid warning and protective system for the capital, but nothing was done.

On January 10 the landings in the Dutch East Indies began. They went well for the Japanese, the juggernaut continued to roll, and even Ugaki, who had a cautious mind, was becoming convinced of the invincibility of the Japanese armed forces. It was easy to do. Radio Tokyo was now claiming openly that one Japanese soldier was worth three enemy soldiers in fighting skill and spirit. The Imperial forces were at the top. There seemed no way they could be defeated, except in one place. The campaign in the Philippines was going very slowly in the Bataan Peninsula. But the hopeful thing from the Japanese point of view was the report that the Americans were running short of food. Admiral Ugaki expected that the rich-living Americans would soon give up.

One problem was already causing troubles for the fleet. At Tarakan the Japanese landed on January 12. The Dutch responded valiantly with firing from their fort, and they sank two minesweepers. Then, when the Dutch surrendered, the army decided it would take over. So there was controversy between army and navy. "There is always competition to be first between the army and the navy on such occasions as this!" Admiral Ugaki wrote. "Though this spirit is not necessarily bad, sometimes it brings undue troubles. The basic reason is that there is some delicate difference between the army's and navy's standpoints that cannot be expressed in words."[20]

On January 12 the submarine *I-8* reported having torpedoed the carrier *Lexington* and sunk her. But the report was wrong. The carrier was the *Saratoga*, and she was not sunk but damaged; she went back to the west coast of the United States and was repaired. But the incident gave a great lift to the Combined Fleet staff because it justified the Japanese use of submarines. This manner of approach to submarines was to continue throughout the war.

By mid-January 1942 Admiral Ugaki had completed the task assigned to him by Admiral Yamamoto, to come up with a plan for Combined Fleet operations after the first phase of the war was complete in March. Ugaki had created a plan for an attack on Midway, Johnston, and Palmyra in June, which would enable the Japanese to build up enormous air strength in the east central Pacific. After that was done they would plan for the invasion of Hawaii. At the same time they would lure the American fleet out of Hawaii and destroy it. Admiral Yamamoto was very emphatic on this point; the American fleet must be destroyed before it could be built into something really powerful that would challenge the Japanese fleet.[21]

Admiral Yamamoto was growing distressed because the navy had followed the army's boastful pattern of dealing with publicity in this war. After the attack on the American carrier, although Admiral Ugaki and the staff of the Combined Fleet could find no evidence of the sinking of a carrier, Tokyo trumpeted the news that the carrier Lexington had been sunk and all the newspapers in Tokyo carried headlines. Ugaki noted in his diary that this was very unfortunate because the navy was not supposed to tell lies.[22]

The string of victories continued. On January 23 the Japanese made successful landings at Rabaul and Kavieng, which extended them into the South Pacific and opened bases for attacks on British New Guinea and Australia. The next day the Japanese landed at Balikpapan and Kendari in the Dutch East Indies, and the fight for control of the Dutch colony was on.

While the Japanese were thus occupied on February 1, the Americans made their first strike at the enemy. A carrier task force raided Wotje, Eniwetok, Kwajalein, and Jaluit. It did not do much damage. Some auxiliary ships were sunk and some installations damaged. But the commander of the Sixth Naval Base Force, Rear Admiral Yashiro Yukichi, was killed and the shock was significant at Combined Fleet headquarters. Immediately Admiral Ugaki ordered many aircraft to the Marshalls and submarines to scour the waters of the central Pacific to keep such an event from recurring. To Admiral Ugaki the shock was personal. Admiral Yukichi was a friend and classmate and roommate from Naval Academy days.[23]

To Yamamoto the most worrisome thing was the surprise element, which meant that it could happen to Japan as well. In the eyes of the navy this was the most significant development of the Pacific war to date, in spite of all the victories, because it presaged the future. Unless something could be done, the quick, clean war that everyone hoped for could not be carried out. And as Admiral Yamamoto had warned Prince Konoye several months before the war started, when Konoye as prime minister had called Yamamoto to Tokyo to seek his advice, the navy could win many victories in the early months of the war and then lose the war because of the strength of the American economy.[24]

—————————————————————————————

In the Coral Sea

The first of the American carrier air raids had an electric effect on the Japanese that was not appreciated in Washington or Pearl Harbor at the time. From the Japanese point of view, the raid was a warning. Admiral Yamamoto immediately took steps to strengthen the Marshalls and other areas, particularly the Japanese home islands, because he expected air raids on Tokyo at any time. To do this he had to pull forces from the south, and this meant an end, for the moment, of any expansion of the war in the south by the navy.[1]

The war in the Dutch East Indies was going very well, although the Japanese were sustaining some casualties in ships and men. In the battle of the Java Sea most of the Allied Combined Fleet was sunk, paving the way for the occupation of Java and Sumatra. These were key islands for the Japanese since they housed the oil refinement centers for the far-flung fields that reached as far as Borneo. All this was very satisfactory to Yamamoto and the staff of the Combined Fleet. Just now their concern was elsewhere. Imperial General Headquarters and the Naval General Staff were taking a very cool attitude toward Yamamoto's plan for attack on Midway and later on Hawaii. They did not seem to place any value on Yamamoto's major concern: the existence and growing strength of the American carrier fleet. Admiral Ugaki sent a staff officer to Tokyo to investigate, and he reported back in early February that no decisions had been reached and that he was using his most persuasive arguments. In Tokyo they seemed to have no plans at all for the future.[2]

This failure of Tokyo to appreciate the realities of the war at sea continued to bother the staff of the Combined Fleet. Admiral Ugaki's sole concern was the establishment of Japanese power. He gave this some thought on February 11, which Japan celebrated as the 2,602nd anniversary of the foundation of the Japanese empire. "We must renew our resolution and with 100 million people of one heart, break through all hardships to accomplish the concept of *hakko ichiu* [all the world under one roof]."[3]

He addressed this issue again on his fifty-second birthday on February 15. "My great ambition is the attainment of the objects of the great East Asia war. If this is done I shall have nothing else to say. . . . I shall renew my resolution to fulfill the heaven-sent mission myself and comfort the souls of the deceased parents." He was, in other words, ready to die at any time. His wife was dead, his children were grown, and he lived only to fulfill his responsibilities as a naval officer.[4]

Operations were going well in the Dutch East Indies, but Admiral Yamamoto was concerned about the Burma area, where the army had also begun an invasion. The British fleet was expected to give some trouble there. Admiral Yamamoto ordered the carrier task force to the Indian Ocean to launch a surprise attack on the British naval bases there.

On February 15 Singapore fell to the Japanese and British General Percival surrendered. Japan erupted in a new wave of euphoria that extended from the throne to the man on the street. The Diet held a special session, although it was in recess, and passed unanimously a vote of thanks to the army and the navy. The Emperor sent rescripts to army and navy commanders:

In close and proper cooperation, the army and navy forces in Malaya successfully carried out the difficult tasks of escort, transportation, and the landing operations. Then, advancing a long way, beating the enemy everywhere, enduring the heat and braving the dangerous jungle, they captured Singapore swiftly and overturned the British foundation in East Asia. I praise them deeply.

The celebration went on for three days, encouraged by the government. The Emperor appeared on his white horse, White Snow, in full general's uniform on the Nijubashi, the public bridge that spans the moat surrounding the Imperial Palace. The Emperor and the Empress also appeared later with the Imperial family to receive the congratulations of notables. The excitement was greater than at any time since the victories in the early days of the China war.[5]

When the Diet reconvened, Prime Minister Tojo spoke glowingly of the promising future of the Greater East Asia Co-Prosperity Sphere. Burma would be built up. Japan would assist India to become independent of Britain. The Dutch East Indies would become Indonesia. He called on Australia and New Zealand to abandon Britain and the United States and join Japan in building a new sort of Pacific system. Imperial General Headquarters changed the name of Singapore to Shonan in commemoration of "the great southern advance of the Yamato nation in the seventeenth year of Showa by capturing Singapore, the citadel of British aggression in the east on its way to establishing a new order in the world."[6]

The headiness of victory continued. On February 19, 1942, the carrier task force struck Darwin and wrecked the town. It also sank several ships in the harbor. The Japanese claimed three destroyers, a subchaser, and eight merchant ships. The claim was high but the Japanese were correct in one assumption that Admiral Ugaki made: "I am sure the Australians were shocked and scared stiff." They were, indeed, half expecting an invasion attempt at any time.[7]

But the Japanese navy was not interested in Australia at that point. The following day aboard the new flagship

Yamato, the Combined Fleet staff held the first "table top exercise" in which replicas of ships were moved around to study the Midway invasion operation that was also supposed to draw the American Pacific Fleet to its destruction.

Meanwhile, victory continued to follow victory. The only shadow was in the Philippines, where the stubborn Americans continued to hold out in Bataan Peninsula. The Dutch East Indies surrendered. So did Rangoon, and on March 12 all Japan celebrated again.

But beneath all the celebration, difficulties and schisms were beginning to appear. The army reacted very badly to Yamamoto's proposal for a two-pronged drive in the eastern Pacific. They did not have the men, said the army, to extend their occupation to Hawaii. They still had to worry about the Russians, and they had to keep the now huge Kwantung Army on the Russian border. Furthermore, General Tojo, who was also minister of war, wanted to use merchant shipping for a while to alleviate some of the more serious civilian shortages, which were beginning to cause unrest around the country.[8]

On March 23 Admiral Ugaki learned that General Douglas MacArthur and his wife and staff had escaped from Corregidor Island to Australia and that MacArthur was calling for support from the United States to defend Australia and carry the war against Japan. Ugaki wondered, in the pages of his diary, whether MacArthur was a great general or a crazy one.[9]

The Japanese were supremely confident. That was the reason for Ugaki's question. They had made a landing on New Guinea, and it had been unopposed. They were mopping up in western New Guinea and waiting confidently for the conquest of the rest of that island. After that, Australia and New Zealand. But first would come Fiji and Samoa.[10]

Japan's conquests had unleashed the American submarines for attack on a far-flung field. In the first days of the war, the staff of the Combined Fleet was contemptuous of the American submarines. They attacked only in pairs, said Admiral

Ugaki, and their attacks were not notable for ferocity. But even by the spring of 1942 the Combined Fleet staff began to have a new attitude about the American submarines, and the proof of it was the formation of the First Escort Force under Vice Admiral Yasuo Inouye to control and manage Japanese convoys. Even with defective torpedoes, about which the Japanese knew nothing, the American submarines were beginning to cost Japan dearly in the sinking of escorted ships.[11]

The Japanese carrier force raided British bases on Ceylon in April and sank several ships, including two cruisers and the old carrier *Hermes*. More important to the Combined Fleet, they drove the British out of the eastern Indian Ocean, giving Japanese forces in Burma full sway.

In April the fall of Bataan brought a welcome relief to the Japanese military installation. The continued holdout of the American forces in the Philippines, months after the date scheduled by Imperial General Headquarters for victory, had been a considerable embarrassment. It cost General Homma, the commander in the Philippines, his career. But by mid-April it was all over on Bataan, and only Corregidor stood, a lonely bastion in East Asia to remind the world that Japanese power was not total. It would hold out a few more weeks, but in the end, without any assistance at all from the United States, General Jonathan Wainwright would have to surrender.

In the interim, on April 18, a rude shock came to the Combined Fleet whose task it was to protect Japan from attack. Tokyo and other cities in Japan were raided by sixteen B-25 medium bombers from an American carrier under the noses of the Combined Fleet. To be sure, the six carriers of the attack force were off completing their mission in Indian Ocean waters. The other carriers were off in various parts of the South Pacific on missions to extend the empire of Japan. There were plenty of land-based aircraft in Japan, but not many that could carry out a search mission seven hundred miles from shore. These were mostly Kawanishi flying boats, and the bomb loads they could carry were limited.

The excitement began aboard the *Yamato* early on April 18 with a telephone call from the chief of the Naval General Staff in Tokyo. Three enemy carriers had been reported by a patrol boat to be 700 miles east of Tokyo. But after making the report the patrol boat had gone off the air and had not been heard from again.

Admiral Yamamoto sent a message to Admiral Nagumo, who was at that point off the shore of Taiwan, telling him to hurry back to Japan and search the area east of Tokyo. But it would be at least a day and a half before the carriers could reach the area, and Yamamoto knew that the enemy carriers would be long gone and far away. The Japanese Second Fleet, lying in Yokosuka harbor, was given the task of searching out the enemy and destroying the ships, but it was a forlorn hope because the Second Fleet had no carriers.

Shortly after lunch the flagship had news of an air raid on Tokyo, but there were no details. It was late afternoon before Admiral Yamamoto was able to round up and send off about fifty planes with long enough range to search the area where the carriers had been sighted, and they found nothing.

That night the flagship had the details of the raid. In Tokyo nine places had been bombed and twelve people had been killed and a hundred wounded. Fifty houses had burned down and fifty more were damaged. The bombers had also struck the Yokosuka naval base, damaging one warship, and they had bombed Nagoya, several places in Wakayama Prefecture, Kawasaki, Kobe, and as far west as Niigata Prefecture. The immediate reaction aboard the flagship was to ride off in all directions. Someone on the staff suggested that the next attack might come from the Aleutian Islands, so naval air searches from Hokkaido north and east were begun. All sorts of other precautions were considered and search planes were in the air around Japan twenty-four hours daily, finding nothing.

In a few days Admiral Ugaki had the full story and laid it out for Admiral Yamamoto. Captured American fliers under torture had finally told the whole story of the raid. It had obviously been a one-time affair involving land-based bombers, which had been sent to take off from the carrier near Japan and then fly to Chinese bases. None of the aircraft had landed safely. But the threat was immense and something had to be done. The navy would watch for the threat from the east, but the army would have to wipe out the air bases the Americans might use to stage raids from China. And the question of the Aleutian Islands now loomed very large in Admiral Yamamoto's mind. He had learned earlier of the American building of an airplane larger and with longer range than the B-17 bomber, and the Aleutian Islands seemed a logical point for air bases from which Japan could be raided.[12]

So, to the plan for an attack on Midway later in the year was added an invasion and occupation of the Aleutian Islands for defensive purposes. The Aleutians would become the northeast corner of the Japanese defense perimeter, which would then extend as far south as New Guinea.

Another result of the bombing attack was a visit from representatives of the Naval General Staff to the flagship to discuss the naval wartime building program. Admiral Yamamoto observed that the attack on the *Prince of Wales* and the *Repulse* had reinforced his view that the day of the battleship was over, and that while Japan had intended to build six battleships of the size of the *Yamato*, no more should be built and the hulls should be converted to carriers. Only one ship was far enough along to be affected, the hull that would eventually be the carrier *Shinano* instead of another *Yamato*-class battleship. Yamamoto and Ugaki also noted the navy's need for aircraft. Under the Japanese system of defense all island areas, including such a large land mass as the Philippines, were the responsibility of the navy to defend. For that reason, Yamamoto thought, the navy should get more than half the aircraft produced by Japanese factories. This was mentioned in the discussions, but even as it was requested Yamamoto knew that with General Tojo as prime minister and war minister and the army in control of the government, there was no chance that this more equitable distribution of aircraft would be achieved.

Then, in the first ten days of May, things began to change for the Combined Fleet. As the windup of the first phase of Japanese expansion, the navy and army had agreed to build bases in the Solomon Islands north of Australia and to occupy the British half of New Guinea. This would be in anticipation of moving farther into the South Pacific in the next phase of operations. On May 3, as the first part of the program, a small task force landed seaplanes and construction materials at Tulagi, a small island off the coast of Florida Island and across the sound from Guadalcanal. They were to construct a seaplane base there as the first stage of fortifying the southern Solomons. An air base at Guadalcanal would be built later. But a monkey wrench was thrown into the Japanese plan the next day when the Tulagi installation was attacked by American carrier planes, which destroyed all the seaplanes on the water, sank one cargo ship, and damaged the other ships in the harbor by strafing.

Also at sea then was the Port Moresby convoy, carrying the troops who would take over this center of Australian colonial rule. But on May 6 planes from the American carriers that were moving around the Coral Sea sank the light carrier *Shoho* and forced the Port Moresby invasion force to scuttle back to the safety of Rabaul on New Britain Island. Admiral Yamamoto ordered his main carrier force, which was guarding the entire operation, to find and attack the American carriers. On May 7 he thought he had succeeded, for planes reported sinking a battleship and damaging another off DeBoine Island. The report was false; the Japanese planes had sunk the destroyer *Sims* and left the oiler *Neosho* in a sinking condition, but that was all. Yamamoto's discomfiture was increased the next day in the first carrier-against-carrier battle of the war, when the Japanese sank the American carrier *Lexington* but only damaged the other American carrier of the force, the *Yorktown*. In that encounter, which the Americans called the battle of the Coral Sea, the carrier *Shokaku* was badly damaged and the *Zuikaku* lost many of her aircraft. But at the end of the day the *Zuikaku* was still in fighting trim and had many of the *Shokaku* planes aboard.

Admiral Shigeyoshi Inouye, commander of the Fourth Fleet and commander in this action, reported that the Japanese had bombed both carriers "which undoubtedly sank." This was too vague for Yamamoto, who demanded details. Of course, the details of the sinking of the *Yorktown* could not be supplied because she was afloat and handling aircraft after temporary repairs to her bombed flight deck. Admiral Yamamoto then ordered Admiral Inouye to press the attack against the remaining American carrier, but Inouye had already broken off contact and the American carrier could not be found by land-based aircraft. Admiral Ugaki and the staff were very angry and wanted Yamamoto to replace Inouye as commander of the Fourth Fleet, but Yamamoto was more restrained and refused to act precipitately. He did write letters to Admiral Inouye and Admiral Sakichi Takagi, commander of the carrier division, pointing out their errors in the battle, but he did not fire anyone.[13]

From Tokyo, Imperial General Headquarters announced a great victory in the Coral Sea with many enemy ships sunk, including one carrier and probably another, but at Hashirajima the Combined Fleet staff knew better. They had been counting on the *Shokaku* and *Zuikaku* for the Midway operation, and now they would not have them. The *Shokaku* had to go into drydock at Truk for major repairs, and the *Zuikaku* had to assemble a whole new air group to replace the lost pilots and planes from the battle of the Coral Sea. So it was no victory. And because of the loss of the *Shoho*, the damage to the two other carriers, and the coming operation against Midway and the Aleutians, no carriers could be spared to protect the Port Moresby invasion fleet, so the troops had to be unloaded at Rabaul and the fleet dispersed to await developments. The Port Moresby operation was delayed. This was the first real Japanese setback of the war, and although Tokyo ignored the fact, aboard the flagship there was a sense of deep disappointment and chagrin.[14]

The Battle of Midway

All during the early spring of 1942 the Combined Fleet was put under an intensive training program by Admiral Yamamoto, although, as in the case of the Pearl Harbor attack, the naval authorities in Tokyo were very slow to approve his plan for the Midway and Aleutians operations. Admiral Ugaki sent emissaries from the Combined Fleet staff to Tokyo several times, but it was not until the Doolittle bombing raid that any sense of urgency pervaded the authorities in Tokyo.

Admiral Yamamoto was more convinced than ever that the only salvation for Japan in this war was to sink the American fleet. The Americans were now beginning to gnaw away at Japanese naval strength. Too many ships were being lost to bombers and submarines. The attack on Midway would help relieve both menaces by depriving the Americans of their forward submarine base. Then, when the attack on Hawaii followed, the Americans, having been deprived of their fleet in the Midway battle, would be forced to send their submarines from the west coast of the United States. This would decrease their effectiveness enormously. Admiral Yamamoto felt that there was not a moment to be lost, and the feeling was intensified on May 2 after the torpedoing of the seaplane tender *Mizuho*, which later sank. Yamamoto was further aroused on May 11 by the torpedoing of the

Okinoshima, flagship of the Seventy-ninth Division, northeast
of Rabaul, by an American submarine; a repair ship that had
gone to her assistance was also torpedoed and sunk.[1]

In the spring conferences and table war games preceding
the Midway operation Admiral Kusaka, the chief of staff of
the striking force, explained Nagumo's theory of operations.
It was to mass the carriers in one area in order to take advantage of the strength of a large air striking force. This was the
"sword theory" of putting all power into one decisive stroke.
At the time Admiral Ugaki felt considerable apprehension
about this theory. And at the same time Admiral Yamaguchi,
commander of the Second Carrier Division (*Hiryu* and
Soryu), told Admiral Ugaki that he had little confidence in
either Nagumo or Kusaka because they lacked boldness.

Playing devil's advocate, Ugaki asked Kusaka what he
would do if an enemy air attack came in or the carriers were
flanked by an enemy fleet while the planes were engaged in
striking Midway. Kusaka replied that they simply would not
let that happen. At the time Ugaki thought it was not an
acceptable answer. Commander Minoru Genda, the air officer of the task force, said he would have two or three
bombers equipped with long-range fuel tanks to extend the
radius of search to 450 miles, which seemed to Ugaki to be a
sensible answer. He felt afterwards that the task force officers
had taken heed of his words of warning.

Still, Admiral Ugaki was not at all sure of the sword
theory. When he had been a teaching officer at the Naval
War College, the popular carrier doctrine at the time called
for carriers to be dispersed so that attacks could be launched
from different directions and so that the entire carrier fleet
could not be hit all at once by attackers. He still adhered to that
theory, although the success of the task force massing at Pearl
Harbor could not be denied. The Nagumo staff was so enam-
ored of that theory that in table war games with Hawaii as a
target of the second stage of the attack in the Central Pacific,

the use of twelve carriers, massed for attack, was postulated.
Ugaki could only shake his head and keep silent.[2]

On May 29, 1942, the Midway invasion force left Japan.
Admiral Ugaki was sure that God had blessed the Combined
Fleet for this mission, but Admiral Yamamoto was nervous.
He considered this to be his major opportunity to deal with
the American fleet. He did not know it, but the coming of the
Japanese to Midway was not going to be a surprise. The
Americans had taken advantage of their breach of the
Japanese naval code and had concluded that an attack was
about to be made and that the target was Midway. They were
also aware of a coming assault on the Aleutians and had
hurried to assemble a naval force to oppose it. But the
Japanese fully expected to have the element of surprise on
their side once more.

The fleet maintained radio silence as they left Japan but
were listening carefully to transmissions from Hawaii and the
Aleutians, and Admiral Ugaki had a strong suspicion that the
Americans knew something was going on. Radio transmissions were very frequent, which indicated something unusual
was occurring. More than 180 radio messages originated in
Hawaii, and 72 of them were tagged "urgent." He speculated
on the matter. Could the Americans have detected the Japanese movement through Bungo Strait into the open sea by
sonar aboard a submarine? Or was it radio intelligence? On
the other hand, it might have been a report from a Russian
vessel. Ugaki was always nervous about the Russians and
their relationship with the American enemy, for the Americans and British were the Russians' allies in the European
war, just as much as the Germans were Japan's allies in both
the European and Pacific wars. The Russian position about
Japan seemed very insecure to Ugaki.

Aboard the flagship, although the ship was involved in the
Midway assault force, the naval business of all Japan was still

a major concern. After the failure at Pearl Harbor, Admiral Yamamoto had ordered new studies made of the use of midget submarines. Now they were being tested again in battle. One group of midget submarines was to be launched from mother submarines into Sydney harbor on May 31, to attack the battleship *Warsprite* and two heavy cruisers there. No report was heard immediately from that force or from the second force operating off Madagascar Island in the Indian Ocean to launch a surprise attack on the British naval forces in that area.

The Midway invasion force was very nervous about possible submarine attack, and a number of "sightings" and anti-submarine attacks were made by airplanes and destroyers. But in fact the fleet was not sighted by the Americans in mid-passage.

On June 1 a radio message was received from naval headquarters in Tokyo reporting on Australian newspaper articles about an attack by midget submarines in Sydney harbor but giving no details. The next day the truth was known: All three of the midget submarines that attacked in the harbor were sunk. Also, in the Indian Ocean two midget submarines attacked a British battleship at Madagascar, but both midgets were sunk and the crews lost. Admiral Ugaki was sorely disappointed because these crews, unlike the ones that had been used in the Hawaii operation on short notice, were highly trained, and much was expected of them. What had gone wrong? It was frustrating for him not to know, especially since the navy had now decided that the use of midget submarines was to be increased in the future.[3]

On June 4 American search planes sighted a dozen transports of the Midway invasion force. That information was relayed to the flagship, and so was the news that in the afternoon nine B-17 bombers attacked that group of ships without doing any damage. From that point on, affairs moved so swiftly that Admiral Ugaki had no time to write in his diary until the Midway operation ended—and he was then writing from the viewpoint of a failed invasion attempt.

Early on the morning of June 4, the Japanese air striking force attacked Midway Island, softening it up for the invading troops who would arrive in a few hours. The first air attack was judged to be insufficient, so a second strike was in preparation when suddenly the Japanese carrier force was surprised by the Americans. In the first American air strike the carriers *Akagi*, *Kaga*, and *Soryu* were set aflame and put into a sinking condition, although two of them took a long time to die. Then the Japanese from the carrier *Hiryu* found the American carrier *Yorktown* and crippled her. She was abandoned and later rescued, and an attempt was made to save her. Then, in the second American air strike, the carrier *Hiryu* was also sunk.

Admiral Ugaki's primary concern was to figure out how the Americans knew that the Japanese were coming so that they could lay in wait for them. Had the enemy sighted the part of the force that came from Saipan, or had they been informed by the Russians, or were there security leaks with the army, or did the Americans deduce something from general radio intelligence? It did not occur to him then that the Americans might have broken the naval code.[4]

But Admiral Ugaki reasoned that the Americans could not have just discovered their coming on June 4; they must have known of it earlier to have their fleet on the Midway scene. Was it perhaps that the Americans were sending a fleet to attack Japan again, and that the ships just happened to encounter the Japanese off Midway?

A few days later the Americans announced that they had anticipated the Japanese attack because it was Japanese practice to follow one move with another quite soon, so after the Coral Sea battle the Americans waited for the other shoe to drop. That was the story patently made up to try to protect the secret of the American breach of the Japanese code.

In his analysis, Admiral Ugaki blamed the defeat on lack of reconnaissance, first by the submarine force. They had sent two flying boats to bomb and make reconnaissance of Pearl Harbor, but they bombed through overcast and did not hit anything but a hillside, and they got no information. It was too bad Japan did not have many more flying boats of that long-range sort or the story might have been different. It might have been different, too, if they had positioned more than one submarine near Midway. But they did not. And the story might have been different if the Japanese had been careful about air search. But Admiral Nagumo was so confident after his string of easy victories that this element of the program was shorted. No one expected that the Americans would have a fleet already in the Midway area. And the Americans attacked at the Japanese striking force's most vulnerable moment, when the planes on deck of the carriers were armed with weapons suitable for attack on land installations and had to be converted to armor piercing and torpedoes for attack against ships. Ugaki considered himself responsible for the failure to make proper use of the submarines, but he faulted Admiral Nagumo and Admiral Kusaka for their failure to make the all-important air searches that would have found the American force in time to avert the disastrous loss of four fleet carriers and all of their planes and most of their pilots.[5]

The loss of the four carriers made it impossible to continue the operation because all that were left with the fleet were the carrier Hosho, with six old-fashioned Nakajima-96 bombers with fixed landing gear, and the carrier Zuiho, with nine fighters and nine bombers. On the other hand, the Americans still had two undamaged carriers, and the Japanese thought they also had two small carriers converted from merchant ships, plus the land-based airplanes from Midway. Besides, the Americans were expected to reinforce the land-based air force from Hawaii by the next day. The Fourth Carrier

Division, which was conducting the Aleutians operation, was ordered south; but it would be June 9 before it could reach the scene, and how long could the landing force be kept at sea?

There was a possibility of a night surface attack; at Admiral Yamamoto's orders, Admiral Ugaki so ordered. But Admiral Nagumo, aboard the carrier, was heading away from the enemy. And then the enemy was lost, and no one knew where the Americans were. At 8:30 that night Admiral Ugaki reached the conclusion that it was going to be impossible to come to grips with the enemy before dawn and that his carriers then would make the difference. So at 9:15 that night, with Admiral Yamamoto concurring, Ugaki called off the night attack and the Japanese turned around and headed back for Japan. Even then their troubles were not over. The Seventh Cruiser Division was withdrawing to the northwest when a submarine was sighted on the surface, and the division made an emergency turn to avoid it. The cruiser *Mogami*, which was fourth in line, hit *Mikuma*, the third ship, with her bow. There was serious damage to the *Mogami*, which slowed and had to be put under escort. She could make only 6 knots.

On June 6 the *Mikuma* and the *Mogami* were heading west, accompanied by two destroyers, when they were attacked by eight B-17 bombers. But no damage was done. On June 7 the two cruisers were attacked by carrier planes and both were hit by bombs. Later that day more bombers came over. The *Mogami* was hit twice and set on fire, and the *Mikuma* was hit by five bombs and went dead in the water. Then an explosion aboard the *Mikuma* damaged her much more, and the destroyer *Akashio* was damaged. It was apparent that the *Mikuma* was doomed.

Admiral Yamamoto then decided that the fleet should head for Wake Island, there to prepare to ambush the enemy with land-based air power. Admiral Ugaki estimated that the Americans had five or six carriers in the Midway area by this time and that they would give chase to the Japanese fleet. Ugaki did not think they would come that close to Wake Island, and he turned out to be right.

The Japanese still had one triumph to come. The carrier *Yorktown* was salvageable, Admiral Frank Jack Fletcher decided, and an attempt was made to save her. But as she was lying waiting for help, with a destroyer alongside, the Japanese submarine *I-168* reported on her and Admiral Yamamoto gave orders to sink her. The *I-168* then torpedoed both the destroyer and the *Yorktown* and sank them both. Six destroyers came after the Japanese submarine like terriers and damaged her severely in depth charge attacks, so that when she came to the surface she could not submerge again. She headed north and made it safely back to Japan.

There was more trouble to come. On the way home the destroyers *Isonami* and *Uranami* collided and the *Isonami* lost 4 feet of her bow, cutting her speed to 11 knots.

On June 10 Admiral Kusaka and several other members of the Nagumo staff were ordered to the flagship to discuss what was to be done to rebuild the carrier fleet. The first thing Kusaka said when he came aboard was, "I don't know the proper words to make my utmost apologies." Ugaki thought that only proper since he blamed their carelessness for the defeat.

Kusaka then apologized to Admiral Yamamoto, admitting that he and Nagumo should really commit suicide but asking for another chance to avenge the past. Yamamoto looked at him and only said "All right" in a way that spoke more than a million words, as Admiral Ugaki put it. He obviously agreed that they should have committed suicide, but he was willing to give them one more chance.[6]

Kusaka and his staff officers then reported on the mission and discussed with Admiral Ugaki their theories of the reason for the defeat. They blamed it on a radio transmission sent to round up ships for fueling. This must have alerted the enemy and given him a position fix, they said.

Kusaka rather lamely remarked that since he had taken the post of chief of staff of the striking force the principle of combat had always been concentrated on a single stroke, after sufficient reconnaissance, and that this system had been eminently successful until the Midway disaster. What Ugaki did not reply was that they had failed to make sufficient reconnaissance on June 4.

Admiral Ugaki did draw lessons from the failure. First, Admiral Yamamoto said the failure was because of concentration of forces.

There were other lessons.

- Radio transmission, even talk between ships on very low power, can carry a long way. The Nagumo force fuel transmission radiogram was picked up by the Combined Fleet main force hundreds of miles away.
- As many search planes as possible should be sent out at dawn on a day when the enemy is near.
- Four carriers should be divided into two groups. If there is a fifth carrier, it should be used exclusively for interceptions of the enemy.
- Searches of the flanks should be made as soon as possible, and re-equipping of aircraft should not be done until it is confirmed that there is no enemy nearby.
- Attack with fighters is preferable, but Nagumo delayed too long. Attack planes alone could do considerable damage. There is no time for indecision, particularly when an enemy task force is known to be near.

But Ugaki summed up the reasons for the Midway defeat into one: overconfidence.

We had become conceited with past success and did not make studies of steps to be taken when an enemy air force appeared on the flank while we were engaged in launching an attack on another target. It was a matter I had worried about and called to their attention repeatedly. Further, Nagumo had failed to make a quick decision.[7]

Having discussed the reasons for the failure, Ugaki told Kusaka that the Combined Fleet staff was not discouraged. They would try Midway again, he said. They would also carry out the Port Moresby operation. But just now they had to re-equip the carrier force, and he wanted Kusaka's advice about that. Kusaka wanted to explain and apologize more, and he did. Ugaki listened and then sent them back to their flagship with 2,000 yen and consolation gifts to ease the pain a little. But Ugaki noted, after they left, that he would know what to do if he had made such a failure. The implication of suicide to accept the responsibility was unmistakable.[8]

On June 14 the Combined Fleet arrived back in Japanese waters in intense fog, and it was 7 o'clock in the evening before they arrived at Hashirajima anchorage.

In spite of his brave words to Admiral Kusaka about the future, Admiral Ugaki was depressed and knew that they would never try the Midway operation again.

The wheat crop on the islands, which had been turning yellow as we left had been harvested and farmers were waiting to plant sweet potatoes. Only seventeen days had elapsed since we left, but quite a change had taken place, not the least was the dreary fact that the number of ships was reduced. We had lost five warships and given up the Midway landing.[9]

It was the first major Japanese setback of the war.

Starting Over

Admiral Ugaki said nothing to Admiral Kusaka regarding ritual suicide for the failures of the striking force, but he had strong feelings on the subject. He concealed them because he was well aware of Admiral Yamamoto's feeling that suicide was a waste of people, but deep inside Ugaki felt that senior officers—commanding admirals—had a deep responsibility and if they failed they owed it to Japan to atone for their failure in the most meaningful way. As for himself, he wrote in his diary, if the Combined Fleet failed he would have to commit *hara-kiri* or become a Buddhist monk. To show his determination to make a new start, he had his hair cut short. For more than twenty years he had worn his hair long, but now he had it trimmed almost down to the skull. The hair he saved in a piece of paper to be used as a memento on the occasion of his death, which he now determined would be either in combat or by suicide if the war was lost. The members of the staff commented. Embarrassed, Admiral Ugaki claimed that it was because of the death while he had been away from his home in Tokyo of his little dog, whom he had loved.[1]

The next few days were spent getting the reports of other elements of the Midway force and passing out compliments where they were due. As to the defeat, it was kept a dark secret in the navy closet, and even Prime Minister Tojo was not told about the disaster for a week. Imperial General Headquarters tried to claim a victory, but the story had a hollow ring. The extent of the disaster was concealed from the Japanese people. Nobody was allowed leave to go home and prattle about the failure. The survivors of the sunken carriers were immediately sent to duty without leave, and some of them were posted overseas so there was no chance they would talk.[2]

On June 16 Vice Admiral Ito, the chief of the Military Affairs Bureau of the navy, and a number of other representatives of the Naval General Staff came to the flagship on a cheering-up mission. They brought a message from Admiral Nagano, the chief of the Naval General Staff. "His Majesty is not concerned much about the recent defeat," Ito told Admiral Yamamoto and Admiral Ugaki. "Such things are to be expected in a war; also, don't hurt morale but just increase your efforts." This was very comforting, because first on Yamamoto's mind and also on Ugaki's was the impression this serious defeat would have on the Emperor.[3]

Some time before, Admiral Ugaki had been asked to write a message in someone's picture album. He had written:

> Sho kyoku zen gan hai sei
> Hai kyoku zen sho sei
>
> Sho sen hyaku sho sha
> Hizen kore zen sha.

> (Victory early, bear in mind defeat
> An early defeat stimulates victory
>
> He who wins with a hundred victories
> Except with virtue, it is meaningless.)

This he considered to be an admonition from heaven.[4]

Ugaki was preoccupied with the defeat for some time. On June 20 a delegation arrived from Tokyo, including Admiral

Takejiro Ohnishi and several officers from the Naval General Staff, to discuss improvements in carriers based on the experiences of those men who had been aboard the four lost carriers at Midway. Admiral Kusaka, of the Nagumo staff, presided at the meeting. There was so much to say that the meeting lasted from 1 o'clock in the afternoon until 10 o'clock at night, and then they had only gotten through the statements of the officers who wanted to make them. The conference reconvened at 8 o'clock the next morning. The conclusion was unanimous: The loss of the four ships had been hastened because they did not have adequate fire control systems.

Besides the ships and many air crews, the Japanese had lost some top aviation commanders. The greatest loss was that of Rear Admiral Tamon Yamaguchi, commander of the Second Carrier Division, which included the *Soryu* and the *Hiryu*. He was flying his flag on the *Hiryu*, and after that ship was disabled and it was apparent that she was going to go down, his entire staff wanted to stay with him and go down with the ship. But he spoke to the staff.

"I will be responsible for the loss of the two ships," he said, "and I shall witness the last of this ship. This is an order. All of you go and serve your country. That is what I ask you to do."

The engineering officer asked if there was not something he could do.

"Nothing, thank you." But then he reconsidered. He handed the engineer his cap. "Maybe you can bring this home," he said.

So the staff of the Second Carrier Division left the ship. They then gave the order to fire a torpedo from the destroyer that took them off, to sink the burning carrier.

Others killed in the loss of the four carriers were Captain Jisaku Okada of the *Kaga*, Captain Tomeo Kaku of the *Hiryu*, and Captain Ryusaku Yanagimoto of the *Soryu*, all of them outstanding men of the Japanese naval aviation circle.[5]

The end of June and July were spent in fumbling. Army

and navy could not agree on a new approach to the war, so nothing was decided. The army decided that an overland attempt must be made on Port Moresby, since the navy was not prepared to start another landing attempt on New Guinea. There was much talk about an invasion of India, but it was all nebulous and nothing was going to happen about that until the following year. Admiral Ugaki learned from some sources that the Americans supposedly knew all about the Japanese Midway plan by the middle of April. He was certain then that the Americans had broken the Japanese naval codes. But no one in authority in Tokyo believed that, so nothing was done about it.

When the army insisted on the Kokoda Trail operation to cross the mountains in New Guinea and attack Port Moresby overland, the navy reluctantly agreed to make an amphibious landing as well.

And then came the bombshell of Guadalcanal.

It was Friday, August 7, and it was raining in Tokyo when at 5:30 in the morning a duty officer awakened Admiral Ugaki with the word that the enemy was attacking the Japanese seaplane base at Tulagi on a large scale. The flagship of the fleet was scheduled to sail for Kure that morning, but the sailing was called off. Admiral Yamamoto and Admiral Ugaki began conferring about what was happening in the south and what was to be done.

The attack came as a complete surprise to the Rabaul command, but it should not have. A warning had been issued two days before after air reconnaissance planes had spotted the American force at sea, but no one had responded to the warning because no one knew where they were bound.[6]

It was not long before they knew that this was a major invasion involving battleships and cruisers bombarding the shore. By about 8 o'clock in the morning they knew there were at least one battleship, three cruisers, a carrier, and fifteen destroyers guarding forty transports. They seemed to have made simultaneous landings at Tulagi and Guadalcanal. At Tulagi all seven seaplanes on the water in the harbor were bombed or set on fire by strafing. Admiral Ugaki and Admiral Yamamoto agreed that this was a serious matter, a large force, and if left unchallenged the force might try to capture Rabaul itself. Yamamoto had been trying with a major naval operation in the Indian Ocean to drive the British entirely from the area, but now he decided to put it off and concentrate on the new threat in the Solomon Islands. Admiral Yamamoto also decided that he would move the Combined Fleet headquarters nearer to the scene of action. Preparations were made to take the flagship *Yamato* and other major elements of the fleet to Truk so that he could more easily supervise operations.[7]

The Japanese reaction was swift. Twenty-seven torpedo bombers, eighteen fighters, and nine dive bombers of the Twenty-fifth Air Flotilla left Rabaul just before 8 o'clock in the morning. The Sixth Cruiser Division left immediately and the Eighteenth Cruiser Division with Admiral Gunichi Mikawa, the commander of the Eighth Fleet aboard the *Chokai*, left that afternoon to bear down on Guadalcanal.[8]

Meanwhile, the Twenty-fifth Air Flotilla planes returned to Rabaul with highly exaggerated accounts of their success in attacking the American fleet there, saying they had sunk two light cruisers and ten transports and had damaged many more ships. Almost all this was in their dreams. But the results of the battle of Savo Island, on the night of August 9, were not. In this battle the Japanese surprised the Allied cruiser force; four cruisers were sunk and one damaged, along with two destroyers. The Mikawa force's cruiser *Chokai* had one turret disabled, the operations room destroyed, and thirty-four dead. The *Aoba* had its No. 12 torpedo tube disabled. So the Japanese force was virtually unhurt. But Admiral Yamamoto had wanted Admiral Mikawa to break up the American invasion, not sink warships. Mikawa withdrew that night, discussing the feasibility of making another attack. But he was afraid of dawn attacks from the three American carriers, which were lurking somewhere in the south. Actually he need not have been afraid, because Admiral Frank Jack Fletcher, in command of the carriers, had fled south rather than fight. After his experience in losing the *Yorktown* at Midway, he was now gun-shy.[9]

Not knowing that, Admiral Mikawa did not go back to Guadalcanal to attack the transports. When Admiral Yamamoto learned this, he was furious. It did not matter that Mikawa had won a signal naval victory. The Americans were still on Guadalcanal and their transports were still afloat. That did matter.

Admiral Yamamoto recognized from the outset the seriousness of the American invasion of Guadalcanal, but his opposite numbers in the army did not. Their first reaction was that this was a naval matter, because the navy had the responsibility of defending island acquisitions to the Empire. The army men also thought the invasion force on Guadalcanal was small, but Yamamoto knew better. It would not take forty transports to bring and supply a small raiding force of the sort the generals thought they faced here. At Imperial General Headquarters and at army headquarters in Rabaul it was felt that the elimination of the Americans on Guadalcanal could be accomplished by a battalion or two of Japanese troops, so that was all they sent. Needless to say, the First Battalion, the Ichiki detachment, which had first been scheduled for the Midway landings, went into Guadalcanal and was decimated in one night of battle. Another detachment was sent, and it was also cut to pieces. Only then did the generals begin to understand that they were facing a real problem. Before they were through they would send more than twenty-five thousand men to Guadalcanal, and fully half of them would die there, mostly from disease and starvation.[10]

Admiral Ugaki and Admiral Yamamoto alternated between

complacency and caution. Ugaki wrote that "all the warships and half the transports I have have been sunk and the fate of the battle has now been settled."[11] But then caution set in and he told the staff to "adjust their judgement" about the results of the naval action.[12] He and Yamamoto also realized that unless they routed the Americans within a few days, they were going to have a difficult time of it. But convincing the army of these truths was something else again.

Even though Admiral Yamamoto was heading for the South Seas, his preoccupations were not resting solely there. The Aleutians expedition, which was supposed to have established the eastern end of the Japanese defense perimeter, had been made very tenuous by the failure to capture Midway. Supplying the Aleutians, it had been expected, would be relatively easy. But now it was found to be not at all easy, and the Americans had sent a considerable naval force and many aircraft to the Aleutians.

After the disastrous battle of Savo Island, Rear Admiral Richmond Kelly Turner, the American amphibious commander, had pulled the transports out of Guadalcanal, virtually abandoning the First Marine Division there—at least for the moment. Because the American carrier commander refused to come up and protect the island, this was necessary. It gave the Japanese the wrong impression that the invasion had been sharply reduced and that only a handful of Americans remained on Guadalcanal and at Tulagi.

"The most urgent thing at present," wrote Admiral Ugaki on August 12, "is to send a troop there to mop up the enemy remnant, rescue the garrison, and fix the airfield. The support force should simultaneously carry out operations as scheduled, while the invasion of Port Moresby and Ocean and Nauru Islands should be completed."[13]

Although Japan had gone to war primarily to secure its oil supply and had taken over the oil of the Dutch East Indies, the military was still short of fuel. Admiral Fukudome, the director of operations, wrote Yamamoto that they would have a serious shortage in November and that the Combined Fleet should take note of that in scheduling any operations.

On August 17 the *Yamato* sailed for Truk. On the way they learned of the wild attack by the Ichiki detachment on Guadalcanal. Colonel Ichiki had been misled to believe that only a few Americans held Guadalcanal; actually the original landing force had been thirteen thousand men. So when Ichiki led his attack to cross the Tenaru River and then intended to move against the airfield, his detachment was virtually wiped out and the colonel burned the regimental colors and killed himself. On August 21 the staff of the Combined Fleet suddenly realized that the American position on Guadalcanal was much stronger than the events at sea in the area had indicated.[14]

Imperial General Headquarters pressed the navy to send the carrier force in to Guadalcanal for a decisive battle that would help the army recapture the island. So the task force set out, and on August 23 it found the enemy, which consisted of the carriers *Enterprise* and *Hornet*, with supporting battleships, cruisers, and destroyers. The Japanese force consisted of the carriers *Shokaku* and *Zuikaku* and the light carrier *Ryujo*, with supporting battleships, cruisers, and destroyers. The *Ryujo* was detached to form a diversionary force with cruisers and destroyers. The Americans found the force and sank the *Ryujo*, while the Japanese found the American force and so damaged the *Hornet* that she later sank. The *Enterprise* was hit by bombs, but she could continue to operate. The *Shokaku* and the *Zuikaku* were damaged. Worst, from the Japanese point of view, they lost 170 planes and their trained crews.

Admiral Ugaki considered the operation to be a failure for the following reasons:

• The Japanese depended too much on search by flying boats, and the time lag of reporting was too great.

- When a float plane of the task force did find the enemy two hundred miles to the south, its report was too late and the Third Fleet, which got the report, did not communicate it to the other units. They had recently revised the codes, so there was a substantial delay in communication.
- The reporting of the enemy position was so full of error that only the first wave of attack planes found them. The fliers should have used the system of search and attack.
- Contact with the enemy was not maintained after the first attack, so a night attack was out of the question.
- The *Ryujo* was used as a decoy but should have had more fighter protection than she did.[15]

The battles around Guadalcanal in the next few days were indecisive and constituted a great source of worry to the Combined Fleet, which wanted to come to grips with the enemy. One problem of dealing with Guadalcanal was the distance from Rabaul. Too many missions never got to the island, being forestalled by bad weather. What was needed was an intermediate base, and one was being prepared at Buka, on the end of Bougainville. But it was not yet ready.

Two small triumphs were made on August 26, 1942, in the capture of Nauru and Ocean islands. They were not very important, but they could serve as air bases for further expansion in the South Pacific, and Ocean Island was valuable for its chemicals. But the problem of the capture of Guadalcanal remained, and it was the most important matter on the navy agenda.

The attrition to the Japanese naval air force was enormous. On August 27 Admiral Ugaki was awakened at 2:00 A.M. with a message from Rabaul. The Twenty-fifth Air Flotilla had lost so many planes in recent days on the Guadalcanal run that its plight was desperate. Ugaki dispatched a small carrier, the *Kasuga Maru*, to the Marshalls to ferry fighters from the Twenty-fourth Air Flotilla there.[16]

Early in September the Combined Fleet sent two staff officers to Rabaul by flying boat to confer with the army and navy commanders there. Two problems had to be sorted out: the Guadalcanal situation and an equally vexing one in New Guinea. In New Guinea the Japanese army had attacked by land across the Kokoda Trail and failed to take New Guinea; this caused the loss of the force commander, who had disappeared into the jungle with a small party that never reappeared.

They went armed with the following considerations by Admiral Ugaki:

• Guadalcanal must be secured by the army. The navy alone could not do it, and the navy air arm could not do it.

• The assault on the Rabi airfield on New Guinea had turned out to be a complete failure. The army must recover its survivors and make a new attempt to take the field.

• The Kokoda Trail adventure had proved a fool's mission. An invasion from the sea was the only way to take Port Moresby, and the planning for this by army and navy must start.[17]

The navy had begun reinforcing Guadalcanal with destroyers, sending troops and supplies almost nightly. This worked fairly well. Sometimes, as on September 2, they were surprised by the Americans and had to suspend operations. But in these days of August and September the Americans were still on the defensive in Guadalcanal, so the supply missions run by Rear Admiral Raizo Tanaka generally succeeded.[18]

In September the Japanese army continued to believe that they could clear the Americans out of Guadalcanal with a handful of troops, so they continued to send in battalion-size detachments. By September three such detachments—the Kawaguchi, Aoba, and Oka—had been sent, to act with the remains of the Ichiki detachment and the survivors of the initial landings by the Americans.

Admiral Ugaki went to Rabaul to discuss these matters. He

told General Hyakutake's staff that this was not nearly enough force with which to do the job, particularly since they had to move through dense jungle to reach the airfield. But the army was so bloated with the victories of the past that the staff paid no attention to Ugaki's words. "We should stop the optimistic thinking and think of countermeasures to meet the situation in case of failure," he told the staff of the Eleventh Air Fleet. "I also communicated this to the army, but both commands were dazed by hope and did not pay much attention to my advice."

After he had argued until he was tired of it, he concluded that the situation was hopeless. The army and Eleventh Air Fleet commands remained optimistic. On September 13 the Aoba and Oka detachments attacked and were met with such stern resistance by the marines that they withdrew south of the airfield. The Kawaguchi detachment announced that it would attack that night.

The next day, Admiral Ugaki had the results from the naval radio station on Guadalcanal. The Kawaguchi detachment reported:

The batteries of the eastern position began firing on the evening of September 12, as scheduled, but the main force was delayed by the difficult march in the jungle and was only able to attack on the 13th. Enemy resistance was unexpectedly strong, so that we suffered great loss, including the battalion commander. We were forced to withdraw. After regrouping the remaining force on the west side of the [Tenaru] River, we are going to plan our move.

All Ugaki could say was that it had turned out just as he had expected.[19]

On September 14 Admiral Ugaki went to the Eleventh Air Fleet headquarters and asked the staff to draft a new plan for the joint attack. Then he went to the army headquarters. There he found the staff in thorough confusion. They had staked everything on the success of the surprise attack by the Kawaguchi detachment, and now they did not know what to do next. He visited the chief of staff of the Seventeenth Army and talked with him for a while, trying to encourage him. For the navy's part, he said, the Combined Fleet would help all it could. The navy would transport the troops to Guadalcanal by destroyer and would bring big ships to shell the airfield and keep the Americans from using it.

From his conversation with the Seventeenth Army chief of staff, Ugaki learned that the misapprehension of the situation on Guadalcanal extended right up to the top of Imperial General Headquarters. Now the Seventeenth Army leaders were so dispirited they had to be persuaded to try again. Ugaki had the feeling that the chief of staff was too weak for his job and should be replaced. As he analyzed the situation on Guadalcanal he came to several conclusions:

First, the Japanese had underestimated the Americans' determination to launch their first offensive, in which President Roosevelt was determined to stake his honor for the congressional election campaign of the fall. They had poured in their fighting strength despite repeated losses. Their defenses on Guadalcanal were thoroughly prepared. Meanwhile, the Japanese had overestimated their own strength and sought success in surprise attack with lightly equipped troops with the "same strength or less" (actually much, much less) than the enemy. From the General Staff of the army in Tokyo on down, they had been overly optimistic.

Second, the Japanese navy had been plagued with bad weather that affected transportation of troops and air operations. The Americans had reinforced their positions despite the bad weather even though it meant taking losses.

Third, the Japanese army had failed to bring in enough field guns and to use them except for staging attacks. Even the anti-aircraft guns that the navy brought in for them were not used. The Kawaguchi, Oka, and Aoba detachments functioned as separate units with no unified command or joint plan of attack.

Fourth, the main unit had chosen the wrong place to launch its attack.

Fifth, a surprise attack can only succeed if it is carried out against an unprepared enemy. The Americans had discovered the Japanese long before they attacked. When the Japanese troops were unexpectedly met by concentrated enemy fire, they became demoralized. They had 200 killed and 450 wounded, and they were cut down to a fighting potential of only 10 percent of their original strength. In short, the Japanese had underestimated the enemy and his fire power. Army and navy should both revise their conception of the enemy for the future. Ugaki wrote all this up for Admiral Yamamoto's perusal and asked that a copy be sent by the army to Imperial General Headquarters.[20]

The longer Ugaki stayed in Rabaul the more depressed he became. On September 15 he learned that B-17s were operating from the Guadalcanal airfield. That meant the Japanese fleet would not be able to move at will but would have to beware of air attack whenever it came near Guadalcanal. Just as Ugaki and Yamamoto had warned, the army's failure to dislodge the Americans in the beginning had created a situation that was becoming more dangerous every day.

Now the foul weather became a constant problem. On September 16 the Eleventh Air Fleet sent torpedo bombers and fighters east to attack an enemy convoy heading for Guadalcanal with supplies, but the weather forced them to turn back. The convoy reached Lingga Roads and unloaded safely.

Before Ugaki left Rabaul, he worked out a new agreement between the Combined Fleet and the Seventeenth Army. As he did so he watched and lamented the lack of communication on vital matters between army and navy. If he were there he would make it a habit to drop in on the army command every few days just for a chat. But he left, knowing that this was not going to happen and that the army and navy would remain as far apart as ever. As if to emphasize the problems, when he got back to the flagship at Truk he received a telegram from Guadalcanal reporting the arrival and unloading of six more transports guarded by a cruiser, two light cruisers, and twelve destroyers. Rabaul reported that it was planning an air raid, but it was called off again because of weather. The Third Destroyer Squadron dashed down from Bougainville, but by the time it arrived at Lingga Roads the convoy had gone.[21]

Ugaki had privately recommended to the navy in Tokyo that the Seventeenth Army needed strengthening. Someone in Tokyo must have been listening, for very shortly the staff was increased and a new senior staff colonel was sent from Tokyo. He arrived along with Colonel Tsuji, an Imperial General Headquarters operations officer who had enormous experience in Malaya and the Philippines, and also enormous influence far beyond his rank. Ugaki welcomed his coming. Now the Seventeenth Army might begin to pull itself together.

In the last days of September the weather was so bad around Guadalcanal that air attacks had to be suspended. The Japanese Support Force, whose task it was to keep the airfield on Guadalcanal unusable, had to go back to Truk to await new orders. Since the resupply destroyers were now being attacked on moonlit nights, Admiral Tanaka suspended the runs except on dark nights. In many ways the war situation was deteriorating for the Japanese, but such was the need that the runs were started again a few days later.[22]

Ugaki conferred with the army officers about the need for more troops on Guadalcanal and the need for five fast transports to bring in the troops.

The Combined Fleet staff began to have a wary distrust of the operational claims of the Eleventh Air Fleet. There came a report on September 28 that the air attack on Guadalcanal had been successful that day, and the Eleventh Air Fleet claimed to have shot down ten of thirty-six fighters that got into the air. But from the naval radio station on Guadalcanal Ugaki learned that thirty-six fighters had taken off from Henderson Field to meet the Japanese attack and that thirty-six fighters had landed. Furthermore, eighteen other planes had

landed on Guadalcanal that day. So much for the Eleventh
Air Fleet claims.

Early in October Vice Admiral Kusaka arrived to replace
Vice Admiral Tsukahara as commander of the Eleventh Air
Fleet. Tsukahara had fallen ill in the sticky Rabaul climate
and was being sent home to join the Naval General Staff. Admiral Kusaka would be an improvement, Admiral Ugaki believed, because in recent months the Eleventh Air Fleet had
suffered from lack of leadership.[23]

The battle at sea for Guadalcanal had definitely become a
battle of attrition. On the night of October 11 off Cape Espe-
rance the Japanese lost the heavy cruiser *Furutaka* and the destroyer *Fubuki*. Admiral Aritomo Goto died of wounds received when his heavy cruiser *Aoba* was seriously damaged.
From this point on there would be naval action nearly every
night as the Japanese fleet attempted to bring in troops and
supplies to the army.

By mid-October the Combined Fleet became aware that
conditions on Guadalcanal were nearly desperate. The
awareness came when the Seventeenth Army moved its headquarters to Guadalcanal and immediately discovered that the
troops there were starving. No one on the army staff had
paid any attention to this problem before. Without thinking,
they had moved troops onto the island without sufficient
rations and equipment. Ugaki had inquired about this situation of logistics when he was at Rabaul, but as with so many
other matters, the army had given him little information.
Now he and Admiral Yamamoto knew the truth, that the
army campaign on Guadalcanal was very badly managed in
every way.

Finally, with the return of Colonel Tsuji to Tokyo, the Imperial General Headquarters began to get a clearer picture of
what the Japanese were up against at Guadalcanal. In the beginning the army was so ill informed about the enemy that
the officers of the Seventeenth Army did not even know what

an American marine was, and they had great contempt for the fighting ability and staying power of their enemies. Now they had learned that the situation was quite different. Tokyo began to take steps to reinforce the units on Guadalcanal. Admiral Ugaki went to Rabaul and the agreement made there called for a joint attack of army, navy, and naval air forces. Only the timing was not then decided. The army had since delayed the timing several times. The Combined Fleet began a series of bombardments of the airfield and other parts of the island, using battleships and cruisers. On the night of October 13, for example, the Third Battleship Division fired 920 shells at Henderson Field. The land-based air force, which had fallen by attrition to fewer than fifty planes, was increased by bringing in more planes from the Marshall Islands. The army at last brought big guns, 15-centimeter howitzers, to the island to bombard the airfield themselves.[24]

The third general offensive on Guadalcanal was to be staged in October. By October 18 the Second Sendai Division under Lieutenant General Masao Maruyama had made its way through the jungle to a point about 1 kilometer from the airfield. They planned the general attack for October 20 but then delayed it until October 22. General Hyakutake sent a message to the Combined Fleet and also to Tokyo: "The time is now ripe for us to engage the enemy once and for all, and this army this morning ordered a general offensive for October 22. We will fight gallantly and expect to respond to His Majesty's wish by annihilating the enemy with one stroke."[25]

But in spite of the brave words, the attack was again postponed and a new date of October 23 was set. This was irritating to the Combined Fleet, for it meant another change in their plans would be necessary. All these changes were costly in terms of fuel and were wearing on the nerves of the officers and men of the ships.

And having postponed the attack until October 23, on that day the army postponed it again until October 24.

By this time Admiral Yamamoto and Admiral Ugaki were

nearly beside themselves. Ugaki observed that the navy had been inflicted with more than enough of this delay, and in the future he proposed to plan naval operations on the basis of the army's attaining its goals on land instead of on the basis of when the army began its attack. But they would now persevere. "We must succeed in recovering the island by hook or by crook this time," he wrote in his diary.[26] This was to be the all-out effort.

But neither Admiral Yamamoto nor Admiral Ugaki really believed the army was going to come up with a victory. They began to communicate better than they had before. Yamamoto showed Ugaki a group of his own poems and poems by the Emperor Meiji about war and peace and life, and Ugaki was impressed; he had not known that his admiral had such depth of feeling.

What they really shared was a sense of doom. Yamamoto wrote to friends that he expected to die in the South Pacific, never to return alive to Japan. He had been having feelings of foreboding ever since he had brought the *Yamato* down to Truk. The war was just not going right. The Americans were showing the tenacity he knew they would show, but they were also showing an ability to recover and produce weapons of war that was even more impressive than he had expected. He told Ugaki more about America, and Ugaki began to have a new appreciation of the futility of this war and a new dedication to death. Only some sort of miracle could bring them through this crisis, the two admirals now agreed. But they were men of conscience, and they were hoping for a miracle that would rescue Japan.

Guadalcanal Disaster

On the night of October 23 the Japanese staged a diversionary attack against the American position on the right bank of the Matanikau River from the north side of Mount Austin. The Oka Regiment was cut to ribbons. Meanwhile the main Japanese force moved up to the point where it was going to start its night attack on October 24 against the airfield. The Americans seemed unaware of what was going on. Admiral Ugaki aboard the flagship had a report from the radio station on Guadalcanal that the Americans could be seen playing tennis on the south end of Henderson Field.

Discussing the long delay and the coming action of the army on Guadalcanal, Commander in Chief Yamamoto observed to Admiral Ugaki, "The one who is waiting for success most will be the Chief of the Army General Staff," because he had promised the Emperor a long time ago that the army would succeed on Guadalcanal.

But Yamamoto was waiting also. His carrier task force was way too far north for his liking, because he wanted Admiral Nagumo to be able to strike the American carriers if they emerged on the scene, and Nagumo, as seemed to be usual these days, was moving in a way to avoid action rather than welcome it. Admiral Ugaki found Nagumo's movements to be deplorable and threatening to the advance force of cruisers and destroyers. After consulting with Admiral Yamamoto, Admiral Ugaki sent a harsh message to Admiral Nagumo ordering him to move south at best speed. He regarded Nagumo's unilateral decision to move north instead of south as a direct disobedience of orders.

Waiting and hoping for success, that night Admiral Ugaki went up on the weather deck and gazed at the moon, wondering what was happening on Guadalcanal. All he knew was that the island had been hit that afternoon by torrential downpours of rain. Ugaki recalled the battle of Okehazama, in which one of Japan's heroes had won a brilliant victory by taking advantage of a dreadful rainstorm to attack.[1]

At 11:35 p.m. came good news. A telegram arrived from the army headquarters. "2100 Banzai," it said.

That brief message meant that the airfield had been captured at 9:00 p.m. So at last the army had achieved success!

"This settled everything," Admiral Ugaki said exultantly. It was a wonderful night. He had just learned that he was being promoted to vice admiral, and now the victory at Guadalcanal seemed all the more sweet. Another message announced that the Kawaguchi detachment had captured the airfield and that the western force was fighting west of the field. He watched the moon some more and checked the incoming messages and the post of the naval forces to be sure that they were in position to follow the army success with naval attacks when the opportunity arose. He went to bed at 2:00 a.m. with an enormous sense of relief.

Not quite three hours later, however, a staff officer awakened him. A new message had come in, saying that as of 2:30 a.m. the airfield had not been captured. What was the matter? That message was followed by silence from Guadalcanal. The morning went by. No messages. The Eleventh Air Fleet sent a reconnaissance plane over the airfield and it reported that fighting was going on around the airfield.

By morning's end it was apparent that the army had failed in its boastful promise to capture the airfield in one brave stroke. But there was still this night to attack again.

After lunch the flagship had another message, reporting that the American position protruding from the south end of the airfield had been captured but that the airfield itself had not. Another signal a little later said the army would resume the attack that night.

At least Admiral Nagumo was now obeying orders and advancing to the south. But his search planes had not found any enemy ships. Admiral Yamamoto ordered the Second Carrier Division to make an attack on Guadalcanal and any ships in the area. Late in the day an enemy force including two battleships and four heavy cruisers was reported, but it was too far off for land-based aircraft to attack and too far from the carrier force as well.

Ugaki went to bed early that night, hoping that the army would redeem itself in the Guadalcanal attack. At 3:40 A.M. he was awakened with bad news. The army had begun the attack at 10:00 P.M. but had found it impossible to break through the American line. It was just as Admiral Ugaki had feared. Failure. The third failure. And when Ugaki sent a message asking what the army planned to do now, there was no reply.[2]

It took two days more before the army command was able to pull itself together enough to plan for the future. On October 26 the chief of staff of the Seventeenth Army sent a message to the Combined Fleet:

In spite of the wholehearted cooperation of your fleet, our attempt to capture the enemy position at Guadalcanal airfield failed, for which I am ashamed of myself. Under the present situation we think we are forced to make a renewed offensive with more strength on a much larger scale, after making thorough preparations. I express my deep gratitude for your earnest cooperation hitherto given to us and hope for further assistance.

To this the Combined Fleet replied:

In reply to your message we appreciate your continued hardships. We are aiming to attain the operational objective with further cooperation in the future. As we intend to comply with your demand as much as possible, please consult the Southeastern Area Force command on practical matters. As we deem it necessary to prevent the use of the airfield, we hope you will continue to attack with concentrated gunfire.[3]

This time the army was really making some changes in its approach. The failure of the Sendai Division in the night attack on October 24 was a real shock to Tokyo, for this was the army's finest fighting division and it had a reputation that went back to the Russo-Japanese War. So the army decided it would have to shift its plans completely if it was to win on Guadalcanal. Two divisions, the Thirty-eighth Division and the Fifty-ninth Division, were organized into the Eighth Area Army under General Hitoshi Imamura, with headquarters at Rabaul. Preparations for a new big offensive were gotten under way immediately.

At sea the battle waxed and waned. The Japanese won more victories, and they lost two battleships. In one engagement the pilots claimed to have sunk four American carriers, which was more than the Americans had in the entire Pacific at that moment. Two Japanese carriers, the *Shokaku* and the *Zuiho*, were badly damaged in one engagement and the American carrier *Hornet* was sunk.

So the navy was winning victories, but the army was not. It was decided between Rabaul and Tokyo that the Second Division was to be withdrawn to the western side of Guadalcanal. The four mountain guns south of the airfield would be left in place and supplied with ammunition to continue to harry the airfield. The two battalions and remains of the Ichiki detachment, south of Koli, would carry out guerrilla warfare as long as their foodstuffs lasted. The area to the left of the Matanikau River was to be recaptured. The navy was to send convoys to bring personnel, ammunition, and provisions for sixty thousand men for twenty days and to move two new divisions to Guadalcanal. Operations would begin in late December after the arrival of the two divisions and the recovery of the Second Division's fighting strength.[4]

But by early November the situation of the Japanese soldiers on Guadalcanal was becoming desperate. The army had not made adequate provision for supplies to begin with, and now the Americans had gained air superiority over the island, which meant the Japanese could not move ships around Guadalcanal in the daylight hours. Their destroyers were inadequate for the job of bringing enough supplies to feed the soldiers, now about twenty-five thousand on the island. Colonel Hattori, the chief of the Operations Section of the General Staff of the army in Tokyo, came down to Guadalcanal on an inspection trip and then returned to Tokyo. He stopped by Truk and told Yamamoto and Ugaki that affairs were much worse on Guadalcanal than anyone outside knew. Fighting strength was down to one-quarter of the men. The others were too weak from disease and hunger to put up any resistance.

And what was to be done?

Nothing could be done until the American control of the air was destroyed. The offensive was set back now to January 20. Army and navy began furiously to try to build air bases farther up in the Solomons. The navy was finishing bases at Buin and Buka.

Admiral Nagumo's performance—and his disobedience of orders at the time of the battle of the Santa Cruz Islands—had been more than Admiral Yamamoto could bear, so he interceded with the naval high command in Tokyo at last to get rid of Nagumo. In November Nagumo was appointed to command the Sasebo Naval Station, which would get him out of a command post in the war, and Vice Admiral Jisaburo Ozawa was given command of the carrier force, now known as the Third Fleet.[5]

On November 12 activity began at Rabaul. The news of the creation of the Eighth Area Army was made public, and the Seventeenth and Eighteenth Armies were beginning to assemble there. Yamamoto and Ugaki made plans to strengthen the Eleventh Air Fleet and give it command of the surface vessels in the Rabaul area. But there was a problem with air forces. *Zuikaku's* repairs, for which she had gone back to Japan, would not be finished until January. *Shokaku* had been harder hit, and her repairs would take until March. Another problem was the rapidly diminishing supply of fuel oil in Japan. It was now down to a million tons, and in the future the Combined Fleet was going to have to secure its oil from the Dutch East Indies.

The battles at sea went on. On November 13, unlucky Friday the thirteenth, the battleship *Hiei* was sunk, a big loss to the Japanese fleet, and the battleship *Kirishima* was damaged in trying to save the *Hiei*. She sank later in the day. The *Kirishima* was also lost.

As of mid-November, the American air control of the Guadalcanal area was complete. The Japanese were suffering severely from a shortage of aircraft, and they were fighting on two air fronts from Rabaul: one in the Guadalcanal area and the other on New Guinea, where the military and naval forces of Japan were fighting a losing battle. As General Imamura prepared to take over command, he assessed the situation and decided he would have to give up Buna, for which the Japanese had fought very hard, because of the inability to resupply and reinforce the Japanese garrison on that side of New Guinea. At Guadalcanal on November 21 five destroyers, two cruisers, and three destroyers escorting two transports appeared off Lunga and began unloading supplies for the marines. There was absolutely nothing the Japanese could do to stop them.[6]

As for their own resupply efforts, they were having great difficulty. In the naval engagements on November 12 and November 14 not only were the two battleships lost, but of the eleven transports that were being escorted to Guadalcanal only four managed to reach the island shore. They were soon set afire by air attacks and were prevented from unloading fully.

"Consequently," wrote Admiral Ugaki, "Our forces there are now facing an acute shortage of food and ammunition. The situation there offers no grounds for optimism."[7]

But the fleet would persevere. They were planning to maintain a supply service by destroyer and also to build forward air bases to neutralize the growing Allied air strength in the area. One such base was to be at Munda Point on New Georgia Island.

Because of the difficulty of supply, the navy decided to try to use submarines for the purpose. The first run was made on November 25. The *I-17* approached the coast but was frightened off by a PT boat. The submarine submerged and tried another point on the coast, but it could not raise any landing craft to take its supplies, so it decamped without unloading.[8]

By November the Seventeenth Army was in a perilous state on Guadalcanal, and the chief of staff pleaded with the navy for resupply and reinforcement. The navy responded with more submarine attempts, but the submarines could carry only a few tons of supplies and had enormous difficulty in making landings. Meanwhile the Allies were sending two transports a day to Guadalcanal loaded with supplies, and their buildup continued.

By the end of November 1942, Admiral Yamamoto and Admiral Ugaki had the feeling that Guadalcanal was lost, at least for the moment, and that they had best devise a new policy to limit losses. Strategically, New Guinea was more important to Japan than Guadalcanal, but the Japanese were very short of transport and the attacks by Allied air forces on ships traveling through the Bismarck Sea were increasing. What was needed was an entirely new approach in the South Pacific and much more military strength.

The problem was that Japan was overextended. Even to bring the Eighteenth Army in to strengthen the Guadalcanal force, the Imperial Army had been forced to bring troops from China.[9]

Now the sensible thing would be to abandon Guadalcanal and concentrate Japanese resources on the conquest of New Guinea, which was needed for protection of the perimeter and also for a move farther south and east. But the great obstacle was the stubborn insistence of the army that they could and would conquer Guadalcanal. Not believing this was possible, at the end of November Admiral Ugaki ordered the Combined Fleet staff to make a study that would show the point at which further expenditure of effort in Guadalcanal would be sheer waste.[10]

Both sides continued to run their supply missions. The Americans sent a transport or two every day or two. The Japanese sent submarines and destroyers. In the last days of November two submarines managed to land about thirty tons of supply at Camimbo.

One of the problems the Japanese navy faced in the South Pacific was the historic army control of its own supply system. The army had its own transport ships and its own sailors to man them. But at any time the army was likely to call for navy destroyer support to protect the convoys. This was often done with virtually no warning, and the navy was expected to drop all projects and perform. Admiral Ugaki was constantly on the watch for army supply activity. Now at the end of November the Combined Fleet radio room picked up an army order to its supply department at Rabaul for troops, food, and ammunition to go to Buna, where some troops were holding out, plus five hundred members of the naval landing party that had arrived weeks before. But the navy had no idea of the extent of the army commitment or what the navy was going to be asked to contribute. At the end of November they sent the Tenth Destroyer Division to escort the transports. On the voyage to Buna the convoy was attacked by half a dozen B-17s, and the destroyer *Shiratsuyu* was hit by a bomb on the bow and flooded. Her speed was slowed to 10 knots. The destroyer *Makigumo* took a bomb in the No. 2 boiler room. Thereupon the entire destroyer division turned back to Rabaul. The transports would have to rely on air protection, and so would the destroyers.[11]

Admiral Yamamoto and Admiral Ugaki were still trying to make some sense of the army policy in the South Pacific so they could adjust navy policy accordingly. After getting nowhere with the Eighth Area Army command at Rabaul, Ugaki posed the question to General Terauchi's staff in Singapore. At the end of the month he had a reply from the chief of staff of the Southern Area Army.

The tentative policy of the Eighth Area Army regarding operations in the Buna area is to reinforce the 21st Brigade and secure Buna, and then destroy the U.S. forces coming from Buna along the coast, after destroying the Australian forces coming over the Stanley range.

With regard to this policy we repeatedly warned the local army that unless we promptly retook the airfields around Buna and other areas, as in Guadalcanal we would be defeated. If and when the enemy airfields are completed, not only will subsequent operations be exceedingly difficult, but there would be a great threat to Rabaul.

The local army asserted that there was no hope of capturing the Emo field with the present Japanese strength, apart from Dobdle Field. Besides, they are showing a great reluctance to transfer the 65th Brigade and a part of the 91st Division on the grounds that any more reinforcement would double the transport difficulties at a time when the army was having a great deal of difficulty resupplying and reinforcing Guadalcanal.

In answer the Southern Area Command is suggesting that if we took the airfields around Buna, secured the area and made it safe for army air forces to advance there, it would be possible to send small transports under strong air protection and to intensify air operations against Port Moresby. Thus the supply difficulties would be alleviated. We are now requesting the prompt capture of the airfields.

But from navy headquarters in Tokyo the Combined Fleet had an entirely different sort of message about the situation.

The Navy Operations Bureau consulted with the Army Operations Bureau of Imperial General Headquarters, and the Army Operations Bureau said that they expected to hold Buna with the present strength and capture the enemy airfields to the south by a sudden attack with the Twenty-first Independent Mixed Brigade, in close connection with the navy troops there. So Yamamoto and Ugaki knew that the army was still holding on to its stubborn insistence that Guadalcanal was more important than New Guinea.[12]

That meant more destroyer supply missions must be undertaken. On November 27 eight destroyers arrived at Shortlands from the Buna area, six of them loaded with supplies, some of them in steel drums. All the reserve torpedoes were removed from these ships, leaving only one torpedo in each tube, thus cutting their fighting effectiveness in half. The two destroyers with no supplies aboard were in fighting trim. On the night of November 29 Admiral Tanaka sent his ships out toward Guadalcanal. On the way they had a report of twelve enemy destroyers and nine transports, and they made ready for action. But their mission was to deliver the supplies, and they were well aware of it. Their unloading point was off Tassafaronga. They were heading toward shore when the lead destroyer *Takanami* announced that it had sighted what appeared to be an enemy ship formation and immediately afterward said that seven destroyers had been sighted. Then the enemy's planes began dropping parachute flares and the Allied vessels attacked. Admiral Tanaka ordered a counterattack. The *Takanami* scored hits with her first salvo and set two more ships afire. *Takanami* began to take casualties, including her captain. The flagship *Naganami* then made an attack at 35 knots. Shells fell all around her, but she was not hit. The Japanese fired torpedoes as quickly as they could, but in thirty minutes the engagement was finished and both sides withdrew from what would go down in history as the battle of Tassafaronga, a clear-cut victory of the Japanese over a mixed force of Allied cruisers. The *Takanami* was lost, but the Allies lost four cruisers and two other cruisers were seriously damaged.

This remarkable performance by the Japanese destroyers, most of them with only half their fighting effectiveness because of the supplies, was ignored by Admiral Yamamoto. What mattered to him was that Admiral Tanaka had failed in his mission to deliver the supplies, and this was becoming the greatest problem that Yamamoto had to face.

On the last day of November, Admiral Ugaki wrote to Admiral Shigeru Fukudome, chief of the Navy Operations Bureau, suggesting that Imperial General Headquarters focus its attention on the New Guinea operations and that Guadalcanal operations be suspended as too wasteful. He and Admiral Yamamoto were more than distressed by the attrition the Combined Fleet was suffering in trying to support army operations that always failed.

So the high command finally reported that the Fifty-first Division would be sent to Rabaul. But it might be too late, because the army unit on the coast at Buna had sent a message asking for help on November 28 and by November 30 had not been heard from again.

As for Guadalcanal, so much difficulty had been encountered by Admiral Tanaka, the officer in charge of the resupply missions from the Shortlands base, that the supply plan was changed to a desperate move. The destroyers would carry their supplies in sealed fifty-gallon oil drums, and these would be roped together and then slipped into the sea off the Guadalcanal shore. The troops would then use small boats to rescue the supplies from the water.[13]

The attempt to supply Guadalcanal was taking all of Admiral Tanaka's efforts, but the Eighth Destroyer Division at Rabaul was trying to supply and reinforce the Buna area of New Guinea at the same time. They left for Buna on December 1 but were shadowed all the way and attacked, so that they managed to land only a part of their reinforcements near the mouth of the Kumusi River.

Preparations for the first of these supply missions were completed on the afternoon of December 3, and Admiral Tanaka left the Shortlands base with ten destroyers. Three of them were ready for action, but seven were loaded with drums of supplies. Shortly after leaving the Shortlands, they were spotted by B-17 bombers and they increased speed to 30 knots. They expected air attack at any moment. Late that afternoon they were attacked by fourteen bombers, seven torpedo bombers, and nine fighters. Twelve Shortlands Zero float planes challenged the enemy. In the fight five Japanese and enemy planes were shot down. The destroyer force maneuvered to evade bombers and torpedo planes, and the only damage was by a near miss on the *Makinami*; it caused casualties but did not stop the destroyer.

The Tanaka force arrived southwest of Savo Island on schedule and approached the coast near Tassafaronga. Shortly after midnight the ships were all unloaded, the seven laden destroyers dumping their drums overboard. The drums were hauled to the shore by the ends of the ropes that bound them together. Then the destroyer crews took in their boats and the ships were off. There was no further opposition, and they made it safely back to base. But they soon learned that of the 1,500 drums unloaded that night, only 310 were picked up by the Japanese. So four-fifths of the effort had been wasted. Admiral Tanaka ordered an investigation into the reasons for the failure, and the reasons reflected the plight of the Japanese on Guadalcanal. There were too few men who had the physical strength to haul in the drums; some of the ropes parted when the drums got stuck on obstacles, and the whole string then floated away. The drums that were not picked up that night were the object of American and other Allied machine gun fire the next morning.[14]

On December 4 the commander of the Eighth Fleet, Admiral Mikawa, arrived at Shortlands aboard his flagship, the *Chokai*. Admiral Tanaka called on him and suggested that the entire enterprise be abandoned as useless and destructive to morale. He recommended that the starving troops immediately be evacuated from Guadalcanal.

But the next day the Tanaka force was increased to thirteen ships and then to fourteen when the new destroyer *Teruzuki* arrived from Japan. Since she weighed 2,500 tons and could make 39 knots, she became the flagship.

On December 7 another attempt was made to supply Guadalcanal using ten destroyers, again transporting drums. They were attacked by carrier-based bombers and fighters, which hit the destroyer *Nowacki* and made her unnavigable. She was taken under tow. But the entire force was prevented from unloading by attacks from torpedo boats and enemy planes. Another failure!

On December 11 eleven more destroyers tried again to supply Guadalcanal. They were attacked by aircraft at sunset but managed to evade the attacks. Then torpedo boats attacked them off Savo Island. They sank three torpedo boats. Seven of the destroyers dropped 1,200 drums of supplies. The flagship *Teruzuki* was hit by a torpedo from a torpedo boat and soon sank. Admiral Tanaka transferred his flag to the *Naganami*. Admiral Tanaka was wounded but refused to admit it because of the bad effect it would have on morale. On December 12 he returned to the Shortlands base to learn that Admiral Yamamoto had discontinued reinforcement efforts because of the moonlit nights. The reinforcement unit would move to Rabaul and begin building up the Munda air base.

On December 15 the destroyers began doing that chore. They returned to Rabaul on December 18 and made five runs to New Georgia in the next seven days. They lost a transport, and one destroyer had to be towed back to base after it collided with the stricken transport.

By mid-December Tokyo began listening to the navy's ideas about what the army must do in the South Pacific. Imperial General Headquarters agreed to the dispatch of two more divisions to the South Pacific: the Twentieth Division

from the Korea Army at Pusan, and the Forty-first Division
from the China Expeditionary Force at Tsingtao. Well and
good, said Admiral Yamamoto. Now let them begin preparing four or five more divisions, because that was what it was
going to take in the South Pacific if Japan wanted to win on
New Guinea and Guadalcanal.[15]

The Americans were supplying their forces on Guadalcanal
virtually every day. So many ships were coming in that Admiral Ugaki stopped making notes about them in his diary; it
was too exhausting a task. At the same time the Japanese
efforts to resupply using their destroyers were becoming less
and less effective and more costly. On one mission the
destroyer *Nowacki* was badly damaged and the *Arashi* was
also damaged. But they continued the mission.

On December 7, the first anniversary of the Pacific war,
Admiral Ugaki prepared a position paper that was going to
be sent to Tokyo. The Combined Fleet had lost 15,000 men
killed in that year, most of them in the New Guinea and Guadalcanal areas. But, Ugaki said, the Americans admitted to a
loss of 17,000 men, which was two thousand more than the
Japanese. He advocated the continuation of operations in the
Solomons and New Guinea but noted that the task would in-
volve the employment of at least five more army divisions.[16]

He contemplated the damage done to the enemy fleets by
Japan, as announced by Imperial General Headquarters:

Battleships, 11 sunk, 9 damaged

Carriers, 11 sunk, 4 damaged

Cruisers, 46 sunk, 19 damaged

Destroyers, 48 sunk, 19 damaged

Submarines, 93 sunk, 58 damaged

Minelayers, 5 sunk, 2 damaged

Minesweepers, 7 sunk, 1 damaged

Gunboats, 8 sunk, 6 damaged

Others, 28 sunk, 29 damaged.

Vessels sunk, 416; captured, 403
Aircraft destroyed, 3,798.

"In looking back to the past year, I regret that we have not gained what we wanted. I pledge myself to accomplish our war aims by good planning and hard fighting in the future."[17]

Comforting thoughts, these, but they did not solve the real problem, which was the difficulty of supplying Guadalcanal. That night seven destroyers went toward Guadalcanal with supplies. They were attacked by patrol craft near the island, as almost always happened these nights. But the attacks were growing stronger, and this time they were joined by aircraft attack, so the destroyers turned back without delivering their supplies.

"The transport attempt by destroyers has become hopeless, too," Admiral Ugaki observed. This was as true of the New Guinea area as it was of the Guadalcanal area. As far as he could see, sea surface communication was virtually cut off, leaving only supply by air and submarine for both areas.

On December 9 Admiral Yamamoto and Admiral Ugaki were briefed by two of their staff officers who had just returned from meetings in Rabaul. It was apparent that the abandonment of Guadalcanal was now inevitable, and the army recognized that fact. That day the Combined Fleet starting its planning for the evacuation of the troops on the island. Meanwhile it was agreed that the destroyers would make one more attempt to supply Guadalcanal and one more to supply the Japanese on New Guinea.

But on Guadalcanal the situation was growing more serious every day. Less than one-third of the troops there were fit for combat. They were suffering 40 to 50 casualties a day from enemy bombing and gunfire, and most of the troops were suffering from malaria and beriberi, which disabled about 150 men a day. The manpower shortage was so severe that 60 seriously ill patients were left in the jungle west of Mt. Austin because they could not spare the 300 stretcher bearers necessary to move them.[18]

In the most recent mission by destroyers, 60 percent of the reinforcements were landed, but only 20 percent of the supplies and ammunition. The men on Guadalcanal were now estimated to have only twenty-two days' supply left on half rations. Known losses admitted by the army to this point were 2,200 killed, 2,400 wounded, and 900 missing. But that did not count those who were dead or dying from disease and hunger.

The only solution that Admiral Ugaki could see was for the Japanese to withdraw to the west to await evacuation. He arranged a special plane for the two staff officers who had reported. They were to go to Tokyo and tell their story to the naval authorities there. A new policy toward Guadalcanal was an absolute must, Admiral Yamamoto had decided. The Combined Fleet would press for the change.[19]

Turning Point: Guadalcanal

If Midway was the point at which Japan's expansion in the Pacific was stopped, Guadalcanal was the point at which the war turned around and the Allies went on the offensive.

The decision was not painted thus by the Japanese military. The defeat of the Japanese Imperial Army on Guadalcanal was disguised as a change of tactics and a matter of reorientation. But Admiral Yamamoto was not fooled. He knew the Americans too well not to understand what was happening and what would happen. He was not privy to the important decision made by President Roosevelt just after the Pearl Harbor attack to put the Pacific war on a back burner and concentrate on the defeat of Hitler. But by the end of 1942 American production had geared up so that more of the sinews of war were being made available in the Pacific as well as in Europe, and from this point on the American buildup would never stop until the end of the war.

Unlike Admiral Yamamoto, Admiral Ugaki shared the Imperial Army's general contempt for westerners as fighting men, with one exception: He respected the firepower of the Americans, although not their fighting spirit, generally speaking. His attitude was the product of his training and the Japanese military mind's total preoccupation with Japanese power and the Japanese way. In a sense Ugaki was a far more

intellectual person than Yamamoto. He was well versed in the
Chinese classics and he was a poet of some ability, which
Yamamoto was not. But Ugaki shared the ingrown nature
and constant introspection of most Japanese, while Yamamoto was almost entirely the extrovert. As such Yamamoto
had a far better understanding of what Japan faced in this war
from now on than did Ugaki and the rest of the staff of the
Combined Fleet and the admirals of the navy.[1]

Even Ugaki sensed in the winter of 1942-43 that Japan was
moving from the offensive to the defensive. He had expected
this to happen, as Yamamoto had known it would unless the
Japanese came to grips with the American fleet at Pearl
Harbor or Midway, which would have bought more time for
Japan. But since Admiral Nagumo had failed on both occasions, through lack of aggressiveness at Pearl Harbor and
carelessness at Midway, there had been no further opportunity to seek the decisive battle for which Yamamoto
yearned. And both Japanese admirals could see that there
would be no such opportunity now.

At Truk, in December, Yamamoto and Ugaki mapped out
what would become the general Japanese defense plan for the
third stage of the war. The first stage had been victory
unalloyed, with only the minor irritation of the long American defense of the Philippines. The second stage had been the
attempt to bring the Americans to bay, at Midway and then
in the succession of naval battles around Guadalcanal. But,
partly again through Admiral Nagumo's timidity, they failed.
In addition, the Americans never concentrated their major
naval resources in the South Pacific; instead, they fought a
holding action there while preparing for their major offen-
sives, which would be across the Central Pacific in 1943.
American air power and not sea power was what held the
Japanese at bay in Guadalcanal—air power, the stubborn
defense of the marines, and the concatenation of errors of the
Japanese Imperial Army on Guadalcanal.[2]

What was necessary now, Ugaki said in a policy paper prepared for Tokyo, was the delineation of a new defense perimeter and the rebuilding of the Japanese naval air forces to protect the far-flung empire. They must wait for the right moment for the decisive battle with the Americans, but they had to conserve resources and rebuild strength as they waited.[3]

What was needed at the moment was a specific and definite policy of the army relative to Guadalcanal. The navy could do no more. If the army wanted Guadalcanal, it was going to take four or five divisions to win it. If they did not wish to invest so much strength, then it was time to evacuate the twenty-five thousand men remaining on the island before they starved to death. Tokyo would have to make that ultimate decision so that the Combined Fleet could plan its next moves.

In December the Tokyo Express continued to run down to Guadalcanal bringing provisions, but the destroyers were harried almost constantly now as they neared the Guadalcanal shore by the growing number of American PT boats. On December 23 the *Teratsuki* was hit and made unnavigable. The crew was put ashore at Guadalcanal or taken aboard the *Naganami*, and the *Teratsuki* was sunk by the Japanese that night. As for the provisions, it was claimed that 1,200 cases were landed, but Admiral Ugaki did not believe it.

As the battle grew more defensive, the navy grew testy with army demands for transportation. The converted carrier *Ryuho* had been dragooned to transport twenty army light bombers scheduled for delivery to New Guinea, but she ran afoul of an American submarine a few hundred miles east of Yokosuka and had to return to Japan for repairs. "Never again," said Admiral Ugaki. In the future the army could ferry its bombers itself or fly them to the south. Thus, as early as the last stages of the Guadalcanal campaign, the Japanese had given up reliance on their carriers and were concentrating instead on the employment of island bases with a transportation network of island hopping to bring planes to the fighting fronts. It was a wasteful and expensive method, largely because army pilots were not trained to fly over water and their navigation was inadequate. But that was how it was going to have to be in a military world that had suddenly begun to contract for Japan, after all those months of unlimited expansion and euphoria.[4]

At least the army was now talking of sending the Forty-first and Twenty-first Divisions south, plus the Fifty-first and Sixth Divisions. From the navy point of view that meant that at last the army was taking a realistic approach to the war in the South Pacific. The attitude was not defeatist, in spite of the setbacks in Guadalcanal and New Guinea. The attitude of the army was still expansionist, and to prove it they were planning the invasion of Wewak on the New Guinea shore for December 18. They wanted navy carrier participation. Admiral Ugaki ordered the carrier *Junyo* to take part.

But on Guadalcanal the state of affairs grew steadily more desperate. On December 13, a lieutenant from the Combined Fleet staff, who had been sent to Guadalcanal as a spotting officer to work with the army and direct naval gunfire in the bombardments of the airfield, returned. He brought a visiting card from Captain Kanae Monzen, commander of the naval garrison on Guadalcanal. He had written on the card.

"Hardships and shortages have reached beyond the limit this time. We have no wine, no cigarettes, severe rationing, no tea, and no salt. But fortunately I am fine and burning with the spirit of revenge." Coming from one of the toughest men in the Japanese navy his complaint showed how desperate affairs had become on the island. But for Captain Monzen there was a chance. As that message was delivered so was another announcing the captain's recall to Rabaul. If he was lucky enough to get aboard a submarine he might now be safe there. And some day Admiral Ugaki could learn what had happened to the case of sake he had sent down to the captain.[5]

The state of affairs on Guadalcanal was confirmed by the staff lieutenant, who brought back aerial photos showing that the Americans now had six airstrips on the island and that all their installations had expanded east from Koli Point.

The time had come, Admiral Ugaki said, when he could no longer see the slightest chance of taking the island away from the Americans. The army had waited too long.[6]

But the invasion of Wewak took place on schedule and was successful. The Japanese had also been building a chain of small bases along the coast of New Britain for barge and small transport shipment of supplies to the Buna area.

By December 20 the Japanese were reduced to trying to supply Guadalcanal by air. The moonlight was bright at night at this time of the month, so the submarine efforts at supply had been cancelled and the destroyers had mostly been diverted to the New Guinea run, trying to shore up the defense of Buna, which was under heavy Allied attack.

From the island of Guadalcanal now came cries of anguish. Messages were sent to Rabaul and to the Combined Fleet saying that the soldiers and sailors would rather charge into the teeth of the enemy and die than starve to death. "It was understandable," Admiral Ugaki wrote in his diary on December 20. "We had tried to prevent such an eventuality, but the tide was hardly stemmed."

All this happened while the Allied naval forces were moving freely about the area and the Japanese fleet was unable to come to grips with them. On December 21 a search plane sighted an enemy fleet 300 miles south of Guadalcanal, but what they were up to the Combined Fleet staff could not figure out.

From Tokyo came messages asking that the Combined Fleet send more ships and make more effort in the supply of Guadalcanal. Obviously the Naval General Staff had not been reading the messages sent over the past few months, which added up to defeat, pure and simple. Even in the matter of air supply, on the night of December 20 the air force managed to deliver only forty parachute drops of food. Submarines managed to unload twenty tons of materials on December 19 and 20, but this was not nearly enough for the thousands of men on the island. The basic problem for resupply had now become the American PT boats that were out every night, ready to take on destroyers or cruisers. Many PT boats were destroyed, but more kept coming in. The Japanese in the South Pacific were beginning to feel the growing power of American might. It was also true in New Guinea, where the Buna campaign of the Allies was reaching a climax. From the Combined Fleet flagship it was distressing that the Japanese air forces were unable to offer more support, for there, as at Guadalcanal, the Allied air forces had now gained superiority.[7]

Belatedly, Imperial General Headquarters was realizing what the Combined Fleet had been saying for months, that the army approach to Guadalcanal had been wrong. Colonel Sanada, the chief of the Operations Section of the Army General Staff, and Major Sejima of that staff came south, stopped off at Truk, and then went to Rabaul and Guadalcanal. They seemed surprised to discover that the army on Guadalcanal was all but defeated. Only a few weeks before the army had refused to accept any such view. Major General Tanaka, chief of the Operations Bureau, had been sacked by Prime Minister Tojo's orders (because Tojo was also war minister) after Tanaka criticized the ministry on the shipping problem and supply of Guadalcanal. Colonel Hattori, chief of the Operations Section of the Bureau, was also fired, although he was perhaps the most knowledgeable man in the army about the true situation on Guadalcanal; he had visited the island several times during the October operations that failed to produce the promised victory and capture of the airfield.

Colonel Sanada and Major Sejima again stopped at Truk on their way back to Tokyo and told the admirals that they were going to recommend the dispatch of ten thousand men in several convoys of replenishment in January, bringing in two divisions to attempt to recapture the island in February. This was heartening news, if more than a little late. The problem now was the American buildup of air power. As things stood, "The problem was how to send them," Admiral Ugaki said. "Did they still see some chance of success, even if troop strength was reduced to half before reaching the island, and even further, to perhaps one-third of the strength after landing?" These days, the Combined Fleet could not guarantee protection against Allied air attack. And once the troops were landed, they could not be deployed with air support. The Eleventh Air Fleet in Rabaul had been so reduced by losses in two theaters, New Guinea and Guadalcanal, that Yamamoto could not guarantee support without air force help. And the problem of army plane effectiveness in flights over water remained a serious one.[8]

On December 27 the news came that the Japanese force at Buna was overwhelmed and destroyed. The same day came word from the chief of staff of the Seventeenth Army on Guadalcanal that the troops were actually starving, keeping alive by eating tree buds, coconuts, and seaweed. The force was so weakened that they could not even send out patrols.

On December 28 Admiral Ugaki received a telegram from Buna, which explained why the defeat had been so quick and so drastic. "It stated that the enemy continued bombardment day and night, spending 1,000 rounds per day and concentrating 2,000 rounds in thirty minutes before an attack." Part of the telegram from the commander at Buna read:

Our positions had been gradually destroyed by the enemy's concentrated fire, but our men tenaciously fought back and inflicted heavy damage on the enemy by charging into the enemy from time to time. Judging from the overall situation of the battle, however, we cannot help admitting that we face doom today or tomorrow.

Then on the night of December 29 came another message from Buna: "We are destroying the radio sets at 1710." A rescue party was on its way from the base at Giruwa, but it could not arrive before the night of December 29. So it was all over at Buna.

As the year came to an end, Admiral Yamamoto and Admiral Ugaki laid their plans for the future and the advice they wanted to give the military leaders in Tokyo. They expected a new agreement to place the emphasis on capturing New Guinea and putting Guadalcanal on a back burner.

A major problem, Yamamoto and Ugaki were finding, was the development of enemy air power in the South and Southwest Pacific. To them, of course, it was all one area, but to the Americans it comprised two different theaters of operation with two separate commands and two separate air forces. Together, the two Allied air forces had totally overpowered the Japanese. Now Admiral Yamamoto hesitated to undertake any further major fleet activity because of the enemy's land-based air power and his own weakness in that regard. On December 30 Rear Admiral Sakamaki, until recently chief of staff of the Eleventh Air Fleet, arrived at Truk on his way back to Japan for a new assignment. He and Yamamoto talked about the problems and brought Admiral Ugaki in.

The basic cause of Japan's current plight was the lack of skill of Japanese pilots, now that almost all of the first-line pilots had been lost in the battle at Coral Sea and Midway and the attrition battle in the South Pacific. The present batch of newcomers had only about one-third the skills of their predecessors. In one newly arrived fighter group at Rabaul, it was found that only sixteen of sixty pilots had experience in the Zero fighter. Most of them had trained in old-fashioned type-96 fighters and had to be retrained as soon as they got to Rabaul.

At this point, Yamamoto's hope for the Combined Fleet was to find a situation in which he could destroy the enemy. Yamamoto had no intention of sacrificing his strength in any more actions that involved enormous attrition, although he saw the necessity of maintaining a naval presence in both the Guadalcanal and New Guinea areas. But the time had passed for the fleet to win a major victory in this area.[9]

On December 30 Admiral Ugaki read a message to the Combined Fleet telling that the army had proposed at the latest government Liaison Conference that Guadalcanal be evacuated. This was indeed good news! The chief of the Operations Bureau of the Naval General Staff, Admiral Fukudome, was coming and so was the chief of operations of the army General Staff. They were to meet with the Combined Fleet and the Southeast Area Fleet, the Eighth Fleet, and the Eighth Area Army. Only the Eighth Area Army had questions. Until the last, the army men at Rabaul did not seem to understand what was happening at Guadalcanal.

As the year 1942 came to an end, Admiral Ugaki mused:

The year 1942 is going to pass tonight. How brilliant was the first stage of operations up to April, and what miserable setbacks since Midway in June! The invasion of Hawaii, Fiji, Samoa, and New Caledonia, liberation of India, and destruction of the British Far Eastern Fleet are all scattered as dreams. Meanwhile, not to speak of capturing Port Moresby, but the recovery of Guadalcanal itself turned out to be impossible.[10]

The year 1943 began. As the high command sent its representatives south to confer on a desperate situation, the men on Guadalcanal continued to starve and die. On January 1 the ration was issued on the island: caramels, two crackers, and a bit of grain. These troops so far from home were praying for food. Most of them were suffering from malaria and hunger and amoebic dysentery, and they were too weak even to walk.

This was the twelfth day of a new general American offensive on Guadalcanal. Artillery shells were falling like rain all around the men. Even the roots of trees were torn up by the artillery shells. This wholesale destruction by artillery was the American way. The Thirty-eighth Division tried to resist the Americans, brandishing their bayonets, but it was like children throwing stones at the enemy. After the assault, the survivors retired to Kamimbo.

When the top officials arrived at Rabaul, they conferred. Again the local army was the only agency that was reluctant to pull out of Guadalcanal, but they were overruled by all the other commands. The evacuation was set for the end of January. It would take that long for the Combined Fleet to assemble its resources for the difficult task of bringing thousands of men out of the island in a few nights, under the noses of the enemy.[11]

At Kamimbo the Japanese troops waited, their plight becoming more desperate every day. Finally the Combined Fleet had its resources pulled together and on the night of February 1, 1943, twenty destroyers arrived from Shortlands. They stood offshore while their boats began moving back and forth to the beach, bringing the half-dead survivors to the ships. Most of the men were so weak they could barely struggle into the boats; some could not and had to be carried. The Thirty-eighth Division stood guard around the perimeter, and the Eleventh Air Fleet had every available fighter plane over the island. The destroyers left well before dawn but were back the following night and other nights, taking off thirteen thousand survivors but leaving twenty-four thousand dead, most of them from disease and starvation. The Thirty-eighth Division came off last, alert to the end. The Americans and their Allies on Guadalcanal, conducting an offensive against ghosts, did not even know for several days that the island had been evacuated. It was one of the most successful retreats in history, and a far better managed military operation than almost anything the Japanese had carried out on Guadalcanal before.[12]

The authorities did their best to hush up the extent of the tragedy. Masanori Ito, a distinguished journalist, gave a lecture at Keizo University in which he described the "strategic retreat" of the Japanese forces on Guadalcanal. He was cautioned by the thought police against breaking the laws concerning defeatist talk. The proper term, said Imperial General Headquarters, was "advance by turning."[13]

But the people of Japan soon knew the truth, no matter how much their leaders tried to conceal it. Guadalcanal became known in Japan thereafter as *shima no gyokusai*—the island of honorable defeat.[14]

Admiral Ugaki and his wife taken shortly before her death in 1940. Courtesy Masa-taka Chihaya.

Admiral Ugaki, addressing Kamikaze pilots just before they set out on a suicide mission from Kanoya Air Base in Kyushu. Note the hachimaki (headbands). Courtesy Masataka Chihaya.

Admiral Ugaki at rest in front of his headquarters at Kanoya Air Base. The headquarters were underground, built in the side of the hill for safety from the almost daily allied air raids. Note the rustic furniture. Courtesy Masataka Chihaya.

Admiral Ugaki in front of the torpedo bomber he would ride to his death at Okinawa on August 15, 1945. Courtesy Masataka Chihaya.

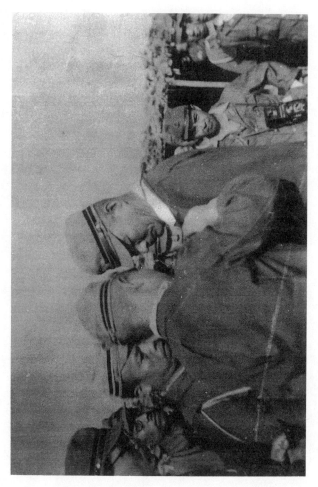

Admiral Ugaki's chief of staff helps him strip insignia from his uniform before his suicide flight. Courtesy Masataka Chihaya.

Admiral Ugaki says goodby to the members of his staff before he leaves on his final mission to Okinawa. In his hand he carries the short samurai sword given him by Admiral Isoroku Yamamoto at the time when Ugaki served as Yamamoto's chief of staff. Courtesy Masataka Chihaya.

Admiral Ugaki in the torpedo bomber he rode to his death at Okinawa, just before takeoff from Kanoya airfield, Kyushu. Courtesy Masataka Chihaya.

The Illusion of Air Power

After Guadalcanal, the Japanese faced the future with more caution but still with confidence in their ability to win a victory in the war against the west. Admiral Yamamoto knew that time was running out. Not long before, a captured American pilot had been asked to name the American aircraft carriers and he rattled off a dozen names, like *Essex* and *Bonhomme Richard*, most of which were totally unfamiliar to Yamamoto and Ugaki. But the fact was that these carriers were not in the South Pacific. Yamamoto felt that if he could force a major battle there, he could still win, particularly after his own carriers came back from repairs in Japan.

The Imperial Army remained supremely confident of its ability to win a war against the west. Together, army and navy planned to make a new assault on New Guinea and then to start back down the Solomons. They had retreated only to New Georgia and Kolombangara that winter, after Guadalcanal.[1]

Army and navy agreed that the first order of business was to wipe out Allied air power that affected both the Solomon Islands and the New Guinea region. This need was emphasized by two sets of events.

First was the new Allied offensive in the southern Solomon Islands that began in February when the Americans landed in the Russell Islands, just north of Guadalcanal. The Russells were not important to the Japanese. They had evacuated them before they left Guadalcanal, but the occupation was an indication of things to come. Admiral Yamamoto was having trouble resupplying the Japanese garrisons on New Georgia and Kolombangara islands because of Allied air and sea attacks, and he told the army they would have to reinforce their garrisons there and add new anti-aircraft weapons. They did so.

Generally speaking, the Japanese reinforced their bases and supplied them only on the nights of the dark of the moon, and that worked quite well. But on March 5, 1943, the destroyers *Murasame* and *Minegumo* in the Shortlands set out for Kolombangara with provisions for the base at Vila. They both were sunk by an American naval task force, one of four such forces operating in the Solomons in this new era of South Pacific warfare.[2]

The second event indicating that change was necessary was the fate of the Japanese Fifty-first Division, one of those brought down at the persuasion of Admiral Yamamoto, which was ordered to New Guinea to begin the new military operation. Seven thousand troops of the division set sail in the first hours of March 1943 in eight transports escorted by eight destroyers and all the air power the Eleventh Air Fleet could put up for them. The convoy was sighted by Allied search planes on March 2, and then the American and Australian air forces from Australia and New Guinea moved in to attack. They assaulted the convoy for three days, and at the end of the attack—all air attack—they had destroyed all the transports and four of the Japanese destroyers, and had shot down twenty-five Japanese planes with a loss of only five planes. They had employed new tactics of skip-bombing, which brought disaster to the Japanese ships and the troops they carried. Half the seven thousand men were lost, and most of the rest landed or swam to the shore without their equipment. The division's mobility and utility were reduced to less than regimental strength.[3]

So in March 1943 at Imperial General Headquarters in

Tokyo the generals and the admirals argued about priorities. The army said that everything should be concentrated on New Guinea now that they no longer had any troops on Guadalcanal. But Admiral Yamamoto sent word to Tokyo that as long as the big air bases were intact and growing on Guadalcanal, the Eleventh Air Fleet was under constant threat and so were Yamamoto's naval operations in the entire South Pacific.

While the arguments went on, Yamamoto concentrated on the rebuilding of the Eleventh Air Fleet, bringing in planes from the Marshalls and from Japan. Finally, after the disaster in the battle of the Bismarck Sea when the naval forces and the Fifty-first Division were decimated by air power alone, the army agreed to a major operation against air bases in New Guinea and Guadalcanal. The army was supposed to take part of the responsibility for this, but Yamamoto knew the army's air efforts would be futile. He built up the Eleventh Air Fleet as quickly as possible and ordered the carriers *Shokaku, Zuikaku, Zuiho, Junyo,* and *Hiyo* down to the South Pacific to help with their planes, which were sent ashore at Rabaul to join the unified attacks. He assembled the largest force of Japanese aircraft yet used in the South Pacific. He and the staff of the Combined Fleet moved down to Rabaul to supervise Operation I, which was to be the decimation of the Allied air forces in the Solomons and New Guinea. This operation had the highest priority with Admiral Yamamoto and the staff. "If and when this attempt failed to attain satisfactory results, there would be no hope of success in the future in this area."[4]

Yamamoto decided to go to Rabaul himself to supervise the operation. It was an unusual step for a commander of the Combined Fleet to move into the front line, but Yamamoto and Ugaki both felt that this sort of action was essential for purposes of morale.

Admiral Yamamoto was convinced that he was not going to survive the South Pacific campaign, and Admiral Ugaki felt it very likely that he, too, would die in battle here. He was prepared for that. In the last few hours at Truk, he assembled several poems he had written expressing his feelings about the anniversary of the death of his wife, Tomoko, three years before and the current state of the war:

From the battlefield I dedicate these to the memory of Tomoko, three years after her death.

Oshimi temo,
kaeranu hana no,
omo kage o
ikusa nakaba ni
wasure e mo sezu.

(Her beautiful face, like a flower out of season,
Can never return, gone forever
Yet I cannot ever forget her,
Even in the middle of a war.)

Tokonatsu no
hana tori dori ni
taori kite
Kimiga mitama ni
kyo zo sasagen.

(In everlasting summer,
various flowers bloom
Coming to pluck them
Now I arrange them for the Emperor.)

Tsue arite
Kyo no nagame ya,
Kiku no hana.

(Walking with a cane
Now I can see from afar
A beautiful chrysanthemum.)

Yashi no ha mo
Tamagushi kawari
Mitama sai.

(Instead of the usual leaves
here we use coconut fronds
in prayers to the dead.)

On gun ya
Kutsuwa narabete,
Fushi no koma

(In the Imperial forces
the bit of discipline
fits both stallion and colt)[5]

Ugaki bundled these poems up and gave them to a staff
officer who was going to Tokyo and would deliver them to
Ugaki's family there. The last poem referred to his pride in his
son, who had just been accepted into studies for the naval
surgical service. Altogether, the poems reaffirmed Ugaki's
readiness to die at any time from now on.

On April 3, 1943, the Combined Fleet staff held a ceremony
aboard the flagship *Yamato* in celebration of the anniversary
of the death of the Emperor Jimmu, the first of the Imperial
line of Japanese emperors. After that ceremony Yamamoto
and the staff flew to Rabaul in two flying boats. By midafter-
noon they had arrived and Yamamoto had broken out his
flag in the Southeast Area Fleet compound. There Yamamoto
met with Admiral Kusaka of the Southeast Area Fleet; Admiral Ozawa, commander of the Third Fleet, the carrier force;
and Admiral Mikawa, commander of the Eighth Fleet. That
day General Imamura, commander of the Eighth Area Army,
also came to call. Everyone was briefed on the plans for
Operation I. After a dinner party, Yamamoto and Ugaki
moved to the hilltop quarters turned over to them by Admiral Mikawa and went to bed early, tired from their wearing
day.

As if to emphasize the need for Operation I, next morning
Allied planes raided Kavieng and bombed the cruiser *Aoba*.
The light cruiser *Sendai* took her in tow, but she flooded so

badly that the attempt to move her to Truk was stopped and a repair ship was sent to Kavieng instead. As far as Admiral Ugaki was concerned, this incident was entirely unnecessary. He had advised the captain of the *Aoba* that an enemy plane had been over Kavieng on a reconnaissance flight on April 3 and that he might expect an air attack, but the captain had ignored the warning. This was the result, the *Aoba* out of action again, having just returned to the South Pacific from a long stay for repairs in Japan.

The weather was not very promising for a major military air operation. A series of strong rain squalls struck Rabaul, beginning before dawn on April 4. But by the time that Yamamoto and Ugaki left their quarters on the hill at 7:45 A.M., the rain had calmed down to a light rainfall.

They visited the headquarters of the Eighth Area Army that morning and conferred with General Imamura and Chief of Staff General Kato. After checking with the meteorologists, they found that the weather front extended all the way down the Solomon chain. This meant that flying the first mission of the new operation on April 5 was going to be very difficult. Admiral Yamamoto decided to delay operations for twenty-four hours in the hope that the weather would clear. This created a certain amount of letdown because by the time the orders were issued, the planes on two of the airfields had completed preparations and were ready to take off for the long flight to Guadalcanal. But Yamamoto felt that the weather would mean heavy losses before they reached the target, so he stuck with the orders.[6]

Yamamoto and Ugaki spent the afternoon making courtesy calls on the other admirals and generals and listening to their views on the coming operation and the war in general. The night weather was fine and starlit, but morning dawned rainy again and caused them to delay the operation until April 7. They knew that this would cause morale problems among the eager young men, but as Ugaki put it, the responsibility of a senior commander was to do what was right and not what was popular.

By the afternoon of April 6 the weather had improved in the south although it was still raining at Rabaul, so Yamamoto decided to let the operation go as scheduled. They drove to the east airfield at 10:45 A.M. and inspected the fighter and bomber crews from the *Zuikaku* who were using this base for Operation I. Then they watched twenty-eight fighters take off for the south. They went back to the headquarters for lunch and then drove to the west airfield. As they drove they went through puddles and flooded roadway, for the rain had begun again on New Britain. By the time they reached the airfield it was flooded with muddy water. Vice Admiral Kakuda, the commander of the Second Carrier Division, ordered the operation to proceed in spite of the rain, and forty-five fighters took off. Three did not make it. Their landing gear failed in the mud. Even as Yamamoto and Ugaki were being shown around the airfield by the senior officers, the fighters began to return and land. They could not get through the weather front around New Britain Island. Now it was necessary to change the plans, but Ugaki discovered that the telephone system from the airfield was out of order, so they had to go back to their headquarters to do the work.[7]

After much trouble they managed to change the plans. The carrier fighters would take off again the next morning, refuel at Ballale air base in the northern Solomons, and then go on from there to Guadalcanal. That meant putting off the time of the concerted attack for an hour, but there was no other way to do it and keep that day's schedule.

That afternoon Admiral Ugaki had word of three enemy cruisers and six destroyers sighted near the Russell Islands, apparently heading up to bombard the Munda airfield. He was not worried. They might bombard Munda this night, but next day they would be the object of attack by the concentrated Japanese air strength. That night radio intelligence reports said there were thirty-one ships in the Guadalcanal area. A reconnaissance flight early in the morning found four cruisers and seven destroyers in the Tulagi area, and about ten or eleven transports at Lingga Roads.[8]

Early on the morning of April 7, the Japanese air strength was sent toward Guadalcanal. Some planes had reached Ballale and Buin air bases, and they sortied from there. Many others left Rabaul early in the morning and met with these advanced base flights. In all, 157 fighters and 71 carrier bombers moved toward Guadalcanal and its clearing weather from the north and from the northeast. Reconnaissance planes circled in the area to report on the results. Soon they had results from Rabaul: One cruiser and four transports off Tulagi and one transport off Lingga Roads were seen burning. This report seemed quite discouraging, but it was soon amplified by others that raised the results until the Japanese thought that 1 cruiser and 1 destroyer were sunk; 2 large transports, 6 medium-sized transports, and 2 small transports were also sunk; and 2 other transports were damaged. The Japanese said that altogether 36 enemy planes were shot down, 24 of them certainly and 12 possibly, with a loss of 12 fighters and 8 bombers.

On April 8 the assault continued, but the weather was so bad that about half the planes assigned did not return to their bases and were assumed to have put down at emergency bases along the way.

On April 8 Yamamoto and Ugaki also had reports from army and navy officers who had recently visited Lae and Salamaua. They came back to say that if the Japanese could put two battalions of fresh troops in there, they could probably win the battle in short order. Yamamoto and Ugaki found that hard to believe. The army was always overly optimistic about its ability to win battles with the use of handfuls of troops. It never seemed to learn.[9]

In connection with the attacks on the Allied bases in the Solomons, the army and navy were to carry out Operation Y as a part of Operation I. This was to drive the Allies from New Guinea air space, and since Guadalcanal was to be socked in the next day, the army and navy prepared for Operation Y. But after conferences, the four weathermen from the Combined Fleet, Third Fleet, Southeast Fleet, and the Eighth Meteorological Corps all agreed that the weather in both areas would be dreadful on April 10 so the attack plans were cancelled.[10]

On Monday, April 12, Admiral Ugaki was sick with dengue fever, but Yamamoto went to the west airfield to see the attack planes off. Before they could take off that morning, the field was raided by B-17 bombers, which set several planes on fire.

The pilots came back from each raid with tales of great success, which were transmitted back to Japan in the reports. Five raids were possible on four days, between April 7 and April 14. Their claims added up to 24 ships sunk, including a cruiser and several destroyers, and 175 aircraft destroyed. On April 14, the last day of the raids, the pilots returned to the Japanese fields to report that they found it almost impossible to find aircraft on the airfields. This was proof positive to Admiral Yamamoto and Admiral Kusaka that the I Go Operation was a roaring success; so it was declared ended on April 16, and Tokyo said it was successful in every way. The Allied air forces had most certainly been knocked out of action, if one could believe the squadron reports. The Emperor sent his congratulations. In the critique that followed, Admiral Ugaki suggested that the Eleventh Air Fleet improve its anti-aircraft techniques and weapons, that more search planes be sent out, and that they cover larger areas. He reminded all concerned that the loss of Guadalcanal had been caused by enemy air power; if they were to win the Solomons back and take control of all New Guinea, they would have to have control of the skies.[11]

Admiral Kusaka, who was very sensitive to any criticism of his air fleet, got into a shouting match with Admiral Ugaki. This left a bad taste in the mouth of Yamamoto. He decided that he would make a trip to the frontline airfields to build up the morale of the Eleventh Air Fleet, which had been badly decimated in the past year's fighting. Plans were made for this unusual trip to several forward airfields, and they were radioed to the commands and to Tokyo. In the course of this planning the Americans got the news too, through their breach of the Japanese codes. Admiral Nimitz circulated Yamamoto's itinerary among several top American admirals with the question, "What shall we do about it?" Admiral Halsey was eager to try ambushing Admiral Yamamoto, but it was a question of such import that it was taken to Navy Commander Admiral King. Even King did not feel competent to make the decision, so it was taken next to Navy Secretary Frank Knox, who took it to President Roosevelt, who approved the idea. Thus it was decided that the Americans would have a try at shooting down Admiral Yamamoto when he went on his victory tour after Operation I Go.[12]

The Death of an Admiral

On April 18, 1943, Admiral Yamamoto and Admiral Ugaki and members of the staff got up early, for they had scheduled a 6:00 A.M. flight to the Shortlands base in two twin-engined bombers. The birds were singing in the trees as the sun began to rise over Rabaul. They had breakfast. Then at 5:30, dressed in khaki uniforms and wearing aviators' boots, they got ready to take off. Since they would be back before nightfall, they took only personal belongings.

At 6 o'clock they were on the airfield and ready to board the planes. As always, by his own orders, Yamamoto and the chief of staff traveled in separate aircraft for safety's sake, and the other members of the staff split up among the two planes. Yamamoto, the fleet secretary, the fleet surgeon, and one staff officer were in one plane. In the second were Admiral Ugaki, the fleet paymaster, and three staff officers.[1]

The planes were escorted by six fighters at about 1,500 feet, flying in close formation. When they passed the east side of Bougainville Island, they dropped down to less than 1,000 feet and flew in over the jungle. The plane captain of Admiral Ugaki's aircraft handed him a piece of paper. "Expect to arrive at Ballale at 7:45," it said. Ugaki looked at his watch. It was 7:30.

At this point the plane that was carrying Admiral Yamamoto suddenly dived down to about a hundred and fifty feet above the jungle top, and Ugaki's plane followed suit. Ugaki asked what had happened. The plane captain answered that it must be some mistake.[2]

But it was no mistake. Up above, the fighter flying top cover had sighted several enemy aircraft and had issued a warning, which was picked up by the captain of Admiral Yamamoto's plane. He had then dived down to the jungle top for safety. The crew of Yamamoto's plane got ready for action. It was reported that twenty-four enemy fighters were up overhead.[3]

By the time the bombers reached treetop level, the Japanese fighters had already engaged the enemy fighters overhead. The bombers made a 90-degree turn to avoid the enemy fighters, but the fighters kept boring in and the bomber crews were hard put to evade them. Yamamoto's plane turned to the right and Ugaki's turned to the left to evade the American fighters.

Then Ugaki caught sight of Yamamoto's plane, which he could see was in trouble, flying just above the top of the jungle and emitting smoke and flame. He grabbed the shoulder of a staff officer and said, "Look at the plane of the commander in chief." All that occurred in about twenty seconds; then Ugaki's plane made a sharp turn to evade the enemy fighters, and he lost sight of Yamamoto's plane.[4]

That was the end. All he saw after that was a spout of black smoke rising up out of the jungle, and he knew that Yamamoto's plane had crashed.

Then Ugaki's bomber came out of the jungle over the sea, and one of the enemy P-38 fighters rushed in to attack. Ugaki could feel the plane vibrate from the enemy bullets that were hitting it as the pilot bored in. Several people inside Ugaki's airplane were already dead from the gunfire, including one staff officer who was lying on a table with his face down and arms outstretched. The pilot of Ugaki's plane tried to get down to sea level and prepared for a crash landing. It was also trailing black smoke at this point. The pilot pulled back on the throttles and pulled the nose of the plane up, but it pancaked into the sea, bounced, and then rolled over to the left. Ugaki was thrown from his seat by the impact and rolled into the passageway between seats. He fell unconscious, then he regained consciousness and found himself floating to the surface. The fuselage of the plane was under water and the right wing was standing straight up. He could not see any other people around him. He saw that he was only about 600 feet from the beach and felt that he could swim that far. He had lost his right boot, and now he kicked off the left boot and began swimming with a slow breast stroke toward the shore. He looked back. The bomber was burning, and he could see no other survivors. As he neared the shore he did see some flotsam from the plane, boxes from the inside of the aircraft. He grabbed one of them with his right hand, but nothing happened. He looked at his hand: It was hanging at an odd angle and dripping blood. His wrist was broken. He then grabbed the box with his left hand and his right arm, and he propelled himself forward with his legs. Then he saw one crew member who was also swimming toward the beach. He yelled at the other man, but the swimmer paid no attention and carried on his swimming toward the beach.[5]

Ugaki then found himself in the grasp of a current, which carried him along parallel to the shore. Then he saw four men come running out of the jungle down to the beach, and he heard rifle shots. Soon he was rescued by the men, one of whom took off his clothes and swam out to bring the admiral in. Except for the crewman who had swum in at the time Ugaki was struggling in the water, the admiral believed he was the only survivor of the crash. He tried to walk when they told him it was a fifteen-minute walk to their barracks, but he collapsed on the beach and had to be carried on a wooden door that was brought up as a stretcher. At the barracks a medical orderly treated his broken wrist. Ugaki

sent the chief pilot, the other survivor, back to the beach to
confirm the site of the wreck, and he also sent a message to
Imperial General Headquarters and to Rabaul announcing
the crash and the loss of Yamamoto and most of the staff.

Then Ugaki learned that there was one other survivor, the
chief paymaster, who had been wounded in the throat and
was at least temporarily blinded. When the fighter planes
landed at Ballale and Buin, they reported the incident. Soon
the chief surgeon of the staff was on his way to Ugaki and the
other two survivors. They were treated and the paymaster
began to recover from his wounds, which were only super-
ficial. They were taken by subchaser to Buin and the base
force command. There Ugaki was moved into the hospital
facility, while the people from the base went into the jungle
to search for Yamamoto's plane. [6]

That same day the site of Yamamoto's plane crash was discovered by search planes, and ground crews were sent in to
see if there were any survivors. The army dispatched a working party from a construction site where a road was being
built on the west side of Bougainville. The work gang arrived
at the site of the crash on April 19. They found Admiral
Yamamoto's body still strapped into the seat, which had been
thrown outside the cabin of the wrecked bomber. He was
grasping his sword by the pommel and had died with great
dignity. A postmortem confirmed the cause of death as two
machine gun bullets, one of which had pierced his jaw and
the other his shoulder. He appeared to have been killed
instantly while in the air.

As for the others, all the bodies were burned, and only that
of the fleet surgeon was easy to identify.

So the flight to raise the morale of the Eleventh Air Fleet
had ended in disaster, with the death of twenty officers and
men, including that of the commander in chief of Japan's
mighty Combined Fleet. [7]

After the fact, Ugaki learned that the Americans had been

increasing their surveillance flights in that area for several days before the attack. If the Japanese had known of this before the event, they might have cancelled Yamamoto's flight, but that is doubtful. Yamamoto had placed great importance on the morale value of this trip.

Admiral Ugaki blamed himself endlessly for the events, but it was obvious that the errors were not of his making. Had their timing been just a few minutes off, they would have missed the American planes completely, because even with extra wing tanks they could remain so far from Guadalcanal for only about ten minutes.[8] From the Japanese point of view it was a negative turn of fate that had brought about the tragedy.

From the American point of view it was a perfectly executed ambush, carried out in spite of great odds, with so little time in which to make the contact with the Japanese bombers and shoot them down in spite of ten-fighter cover. How it had all come about was the subject of investigation back in Tokyo, but no satisfactory answers were found. Some members of the Imperial General Staff suggested that the enemy must have broken the Japanese naval codes, but Admiral Ugaki was among those who finally rejected that theory and put it all down to bad luck.

In fact, the truth did become known. Several war correspondents were on Guadalcanal during the mission; when it returned, suddenly the staff of the Guadalcanal air force realized that this story was potential dynamite. Admiral Halsey at Espiritu Santo ordered a censorship clamp on all material involved, but an Australian photographer who was returning to Sydney broke the story in the Australian newspapers. It seeped out to Argentina, where it was played up in the neutral press. Japan's Domei news service had access to this press and reported the story, but when it got to Tokyo it was rejected by Imperial General Headquarters as a fabrication made by the enemy to cause confusion. So the naval codes were retained. Although the Americans had taken a great chance and had, in fact, risked sacrificing the great advantage of "reading the enemy mail" by the ambush of Admiral Yamamoto, from their point of view no harm resulted. The American submarine force, which was the greatest recipient of information about Japanese ship movements, continued to have the information all during the rest of the war.[9]

Admiral Yamamoto's body was carried out of the jungle and cremated there in the South Pacific. The ashes were then reverently carried back to Japan in state on the destroyer *Yugamo* and to Tokyo for a state funeral befitting so honored and honorable a man. The Emperor awarded Admiral Yamamoto the Order of the Chrysanthemum, first class, and promoted him to the rank of fleet admiral, which was held by none other in Japan.

After the state funeral in Tokyo the admiral's ashes were divided into two parts. One part was taken by his widow to the Tama cemetery in Tokyo. The other half went to the Yamamoto family in Nagaoka, a family that the Japanese naval officer had joined in his youth, thus forsaking legally the Takano family into which he had been born.[10]

The nation mourned its greatest naval hero, but the war went on. Admiral Yamamoto was replaced as commander of the Combined Fleet by Admiral Mineichi Koga, who prepared for "the decisive battle" that Yamamoto had sought. But Koga did not actively seek it at the two times he might have achieved it, at the Gilberts Islands invasion of November 1943 and the Marshall Islands invasion of February 1944. Admiral Koga was appointed chief of the Combined Fleet, Yamamoto's staff was supplanted by a new one, and Admiral Ugaki was appointed commander of Battleship Division One of the Combined Fleet, which included the two superbattleships *Yamato* and *Musashi*. Since the *Musashi* was a more comfortable and slightly more modern ship than the *Yamato*, Ugaki chose that as his flagship.[11]

Vice Admiral Shigero Fukudome succeeded Admiral Ugaki as chief of staff of the Combined Fleet. It was his luck, and that of the Japanese Imperial Navy, to have history almost repeat itself in the spring of 1944.

As the Allies moved through the Central Pacific, the Japanese contracted the perimeter of their defense zone. At the time of the Marshalls invasion, they had abandoned Truk as their forward naval base in favor of Palau, which was much closer to the Philippines and to the Japanese homeland. The line ran from the Marianas to the western Caroline Islands and to the Philippines. In March 1944 the Japanese scout planes reported an Allied task force heading along the northern end of New Guinea. Thereupon Admiral Koga decided to transfer his headquarters from Palau to Davao in the Philippines. For the hurried transfer he embarked the staff in two flying boats. As was the naval custom, he rode in one flying boat and Chief of Staff Fukudome rode in the other with part of the staff. Koga's plane was lost in a violent storm, but Fukudome's plane survived. Admiral Fukudome became the second Japanese Combined Fleet staff chief to survive his commander. As it would turn out, Fukudome and Ugaki would both play major roles in the final defense of the Japanese Empire, although they would be on entirely different sides of the argument about the use of the Japanese air forces in that defense when the time came in the autumn of 1944.[12]

Seeking the Decisive Battle

Admiral Yamamoto died on April 18, 1943, and Admiral Ugaki, who had suffered a fractured wrist, internal injuries, and broken ribs, was brought home and put in the hospital in Tokyo. There he spent the next nine months recuperating from his wounds and from the fever that had bothered him since the days in Truk. After his assignment to the leadership of the Japanese battleships, Admiral Ugaki continued to serve with the fleet, but now his objective was to win a fleet engagement with the enemy on the surface. After the winter of 1944 this was sought by the Japanese, but the Americans remained elusive as they pursued their plans to carry the war across the Central Pacific to Japan.[1]

Before his death in the spring of 1944, Admiral Koga had reorganized the Combined Fleet. Such a move was overdue because the attrition of the past two years had changed the nature of that fleet. No longer did it have the great carrier power that could overwhelm the Americans. In fact, the strengths of the two nations' carrier forces were just about reversed compared to the time of Pearl Harbor. The Americans could put into play fifteen fleet and light carriers, plus a large number of escort carriers, while the Japanese could employ six carriers, the carrier strength of the Mobile Fleet. For air strength the Japanese had counted on land-based naval air forces. In their naval reorganization they expanded these air forces, using the island of Tinian in the Marianas as their main base. The idea was that the Combined Fleet head-quarters would move to Saipan; with Tinian being the major air center, the Combined Fleet would run a shuttle operation in any coming air battle, using carriers and island bases to move planes back and forth. Thus the carriers' strength would be doubled in terms of action, and the disparity between Japanese and American naval air power would be eliminated. On paper it looked like a fine plan.[2]

Beginning in April 1944, the Allies conducted so many offensive operations that the Japanese fleet was hard put to keep up with the planning. Truk was attacked twice and wiped out as a major base. Hollandia was invaded on April 3; Biak was invaded in May. The Japanese hardly knew where to turn next. Would the Americans and Australians hit in the Philippines or in the Dutch East Indies? Or would they go for Saipan in the Marianas?

Following the death of Admiral Koga, Admiral Soemu Toyoda became chief of the Combined Fleet. On May 21, 1943, while he was in the naval hospital, Admiral Ugaki was officially relieved as chief of staff of the Combined Fleet, and his Naval Academy classmate, Vice Admiral Fukudome, was appointed to the post. So as Admiral Fukudome and Admiral Koga had reorganized the fleet, Admiral Ugaki was com-pletely out of action.

When he came out of the hospital in the winter of 1944, he faced a different world and a different war. In the interim, the Allies had taken the Gilbert Islands and the Marshalls. Admi-ral Halsey had landed marines on Bougainville, and they had established air bases in the central section of the island. This move effectively destroyed the importance of both the Short-lands base and Rabaul. New Guinea was fast falling into the hands of the Allies. All the places that Admiral Ugaki had considered part of the Japanese perimeter were threatened. The war had turned around and Japan was on the defensive.

On February 22, 1944, Vice Admiral Ugaki was appointed to command Battleship Division One of the Combined Fleet. However, the operating fleet was no longer known by that name.[3]

In the early months of 1944, Admiral Toyoda reorganized the Japanese fighting fleet. The new operational unit was the First Mobile Fleet, commanded by Admiral Ozawa in the carrier *Taiho*. It consisted of Carrier Division One, which included the carriers *Taiho*, *Zuikaku*, and *Shokaku*; Carrier Division Two, under Rear Admiral Takaji Joshima, which included the carriers *Junyo*, *Hiyo*, and *Ryuho*; and Carrier Division Three, under Rear Admiral Sueo Obayashi, with the carriers *Chitose*, *Chiyoda*, and *Zuiho*. Its escorts were two light cruisers and ten destroyers. The surface element of the fleet was the Second Fleet, under Vice Admiral Takeo Kurita in the cruiser *Atago*. It consisted of Admiral Ugaki's Battleship Division One, the *Yamato*, *Musashi*, and *Nagato*; Battleship Division Two, the *Kongo* and *Haruna*; three divisions of cruisers; and one destroyer squadron.[4]

Besides this formidable force, the Japanese navy had a new First Air Fleet at Tinian under Vice Admiral Kakuji Kakuta. More than 1,500 aircraft were to be distributed among Tinian, Guam, Saipan, Rota, Iwo Jima, Yap, and Palau. These aircraft were responsible for the protection of the Inner South Seas, and they were to support Admiral Ozawa's fleet with its 450 planes. This air fleet was regarded as the most powerful air element in the Japanese navy.

Admiral Ugaki left Japan just after his appointment to join his ship command. First he flew to Sumatra and then to Lingga Roads, where the battleships were anchored. To some it might have been a letdown to go from first being chief of staff to the commander of the Combined Fleet and then back to a subordinate sea command. But there was good reason for it. Admiral Ugaki was a senior officer of the naval air force, and in the shrinking world of Japanese air power there were not enough jobs to go around. He might have expected a po-

sition such as Admiral Ozawa's; but there was only one striking force left in the Japanese navy, and with the shortage of
carriers there was no way of building another. In fact,
Admiral Ugaki was lucky to get the command that he did. It
was an indication of the high respect in which he was held in
the circles of naval authority.

Admiral Ugaki was pleased to be back at sea, for it might
give him the opportunity he sought now, to die in battle in
the service of Emperor and nation. He had no concerns any
more about his family. His wife was only a memory, all his
children were grown, and his eldest son was preparing for a
career in naval medicine. There was no one to be left deso-
lated when he died. And now, particularly after Admiral
Yamamoto's death in action, Admiral Ugaki was determined
to die in service.

There were several false starts from Lingga Roads, heading
for what the Japanese hoped would be the decisive battle with
the American fleet.[5]

All that spring the Japanese waited, wondering when they
would be able to come to grips with the American fleet. By
May, Admiral Toyoda was facing two problems: indecision
about where the battle would be fought, and the need to
base his major fleet elements near the supply of fuel. There
was a shortage of fuel farther north, caused by the American
submarine war that had sunk so many tankers. The Mobile
Fleet had moved from the Singapore area to Tawi Tawi to be
close to the oil supply.

Under the reorganized fleet the battleships would be united
with the aircraft carriers to oppose the enemy. The battleships would escort and protect the carriers, which would
carry the major offensive weapon: the planes that would
attack the enemy.

But where would the enemy attack?

When the Allies landed at Biak on May 27, the navy section of Imperial General Headquarters reacted with great

swiftness. It ordered the Twenty-third Air Flotilla strengthened by fifty airplanes, with forty more to come very soon afterward. Four days later another seventy-five aircraft were ordered to the area. Besides this move, the Combined Fleet drew an action plan called Operation Kon, which called for transport of troops by warship to Biak to defend that place against the Allied invasion.

On June 1, however, there was further cause for confusion. The Americans had been attacking from the air not only Biak but Saipan, Tinian, and Iwo Jima. They had based at Majuro in the Marshall Islands an enormous concentration of forces, which was discovered that day by a Japanese pilot flying a long-range search mission. Thus, aboard the Combined Fleet flagship *Oyodo* in Tokyo Bay the discussions began all over again. Where would the enemy attack? It could be either north of Australia, at Saipan, or at Palau. So Operation A was planned, which could occur anywhere from the Central Pacific to the Philippines or north of Australia. It was a huge area to watch. How could the fleet be ready for action anywhere?

This was the major problem. Half the staff of the Combined Fleet had decided that the main front would come in the Palau area. Most of the others thought the attack would come in the Australia area. Only one member of the staff, Commander Chikataka Nakajima, the staff intelligence officer, said it was going to come at Saipan.

But Biak was voted the most likely place to bring the enemy fleet into battle, so the effort was to be made to recapture Biak in Operation Kon.[6]

On June 3 orders were issued for the battle, and Admiral Ugaki and the other commanders of the units of the Mobile Fleet prepared to move. Admiral Kurita, commander of the entire battleship attack force, had brought them to Tawi Tawi, which was equidistant from Biak and Palau. But the battleships never did see action because the American naval forces appeared 170 miles east of Guam on June 11.

That day the Americans launched simultaneous attacks on Saipan, Tinian, Guam, and Rota, followed by more attacks the next day on the same targets.

Operation Kon failed to reinforce the Japanese at Biak. On June 10, 1944, Admiral Ugaki was ordered into action with the *Musashi* and the *Yamato*. Riding in the *Yamato*, Admiral Ugaki left Tawi Tawi at 4 o'clock on the afternoon of June 10. A day later his force was assembled at Bataan and planning to move to Biak on June 15. But now what Admiral Yamamoto had feared so long ago actually happened. The Americans were now strong enough to attack in two places at the same time. Admiral Thomas Kinkaid's Seventh Fleet was attacking Biak. At the same time the Central Pacific Force, built around the Fifth Fleet, was preparing to attack the Marianas, invading Saipan first. Carrier planes raided Guam and Saipan on June 11 and again on June 12. In Tokyo Admiral Toyoda was sure that the Marianas were now going to be invaded, and this gave him the opportunity to initiate the major battle the Japanese sought.[7]

On June 12, as Admiral Ugaki wanted to go into battle with his superbattleships, the orders were changed in Tokyo and he hurried with his battleships and cruisers to join Admiral Ozawa in the Philippine Sea. They joined Admiral Ozawa's ships, and at 3 o'clock on the afternoon of June 18 they arrived in a position 500 miles west of Saipan. Admiral Ozawa sent scout planes out in every direction looking for the American fleet. Altogether he employed 42 scout aircraft and was soon rewarded with the news that they had sighted four groups of American ships in the Saipan area, which included eleven carriers. The presence of so many carriers indicated that the American fleet was there in force and should be ready for the decisive battle.

Ozawa did not know it, but what Admiral Yamamoto had feared had now come to pass. The American forces outnumbered the Japanese by 3 to 1. They had 7 fleet carriers, 8 light carriers, and 14 escort carriers, plus 14 battleships and many cruisers and destroyers, a total force of 154 warships. In terms of might alone the Japanese were overwhelmed. They had only 9 carriers with 380 operational aircraft aboard, to the enemy's 891 aircraft. But Ozawa had an advantage: The Japanese planes had a range of at least 400 miles, while the American planes had a range of less than 300 miles. That meant Ozawa could strike before the enemy could reach him.[8]

Admiral Ozawa's planes found the Americans long before the Americans found the Japanese fleet. Ozawa launched his first attack wave from a distance of 380 miles and his second attack wave from about 250 miles, as he headed toward the American fleet. The first attack wave of 129 planes left the carriers at 7:30 in the morning on June 19, 1944. The second attack group, launched at 10 o'clock, consisted of 82 aircraft.

But the Japanese had some very bad luck. The Americans had not found the fleet and did not know they were going to be attacked that morning. But they did send a large force of aircraft out to attack airfields on Guam, and that force was in the air when word of the Japanese attack was received. It was much easier for the Americans to send the planes already in the air to intercept the Japanese attack than it would have been to start launching a defensive screen. Thus, the Japanese first attack was met head on long before it even approached the American fleet, and most of the planes were shot down. The victory in this case was really for the American radar, which had detected the coming of the attack a long time before it could arrive.[9]

The first damage in the battle to the Japanese ships was caused not by the air attackers, who still had not found the Japanese fleet by early afternoon, but by the American submarine *Albacore*, which torpedoed the 32,000-ton flagship carrier *Taiho* and did so much damage that six hours later she sank. The American submarine *Cavalla* torpedoed the carrier *Shokaku*, and she sank three hours later. So, of the three fleet carriers Japan had in the battle, two were sunk by submarines. Only the big carrier *Zuikaku* was left before the Americans had a chance to launch an air strike. That air strike arrived late in the afternoon, and the American planes sank the carrier *Hiyo*, which had been disabled by another submarine torpedo. The American planes also damaged the *Zuikaku, Junyo, Ryuho,* and *Chiyoda.* At the end of the day, the Japanese had fewer than a hundred carrier planes left, and all their carriers were sunk or damaged. That night from Tokyo, Admiral Toyoda ordered the Japanese fleet to withdraw. Admiral Ozawa did send the carriers away, but he ordered the Japanese Second Fleet (which meant the battleships and cruisers) to make a night attack on the Americans. So it seemed that Admiral Ugaki and his two new battleships, the *Yamato* and the *Musashi*, might be a decisive factor in the battle. But after the American air attack, Admiral Kurita ordered the Second Fleet also to turn around and head back to Japan; the battleships never fired their guns. On June 24 the Mobile Fleet anchored in Hashirajima and Ugaki was back in familiar territory—but in what a different position! When he had last left Hashirajima, the *Yamato* had steamed proudly out for the South Pacific to supervise the recapture of Guadalcanal. All that had failed and now Japanese naval air power had been reduced to a shadow. Japan had one fleet carrier left, and two light carriers, with fewer than one hundred aircraft. There was no way the carrier force could be rebuilt, for Japan was running short of vital materials. It would be months before the naval air force could be brought back to strength. Even so, the training programs were not producing first-class pilots, and there were only a handful of these left in the naval air force.[10]

Following the defeat of the Japanese fleet in this battle of the Philippine Sea, there was no way that Saipan and Tinian could be held, so the advance base of the Combined Fleet was lost. In the land battles that followed, Admiral Nagumo and his entire staff were lost too, and the land-based naval air force was reduced to shambles.

Admiral Ugaki remained in command of the First Battleship Division, but the Mobile Fleet was virtually disbanded. Admiral Ozawa remained to command what was left of the carrier force, but his chief of staff, Admiral Fukudome, was sent to Kyushu to build up the Sixth Base Air Force and move it to Taiwan, where it would become a major element in the new defense of the Japanese Empire. Now that the carrier fleet had been destroyed for all practical purposes, the Japanese navy was reacting by turning to island defenses to use land-based air forces as they had previously used the carriers. The surface fleet, now commanded by Admiral Kurita, became the only strength of the Imperial Navy. It was sent south to Lingga Roads again that summer, because there was not enough fuel to keep both the battleships and cruisers and the remnants of the carrier fleet in Japanese waters. How the war had turned around![11]

Back at Lingga Roads, Admiral Ugaki spent the rest of the summer of 1944 supervising the intensive training of the officers and men of his battleship division. Much of the training was conducted ashore, for here the fuel shortage was not severe and the ships were able to go out on sea training exercises.

The work was thorough and exhausting. It was so hot in Lingga Bay and the sea water so warm that the men were reminded of Japanese hot springs. From the highest vantage point above the sandy beach, all that Admiral Ugaki could see was a forest of palm trees extending in every direction, waving in the heat. The heat and the intensive training put the men into an extremely combative mood; Ugaki could not recall when the officers and men had hated the enemy more. Physical conditions might be dreadful here by the equator, but the men's fighting spirit had never been better.

They practiced artillery dueling and every sort of maneuver, on land and on sea, indulging in exercises that utilized every strategy that could be considered, and they had no concern for fuel. The exercises of Admiral Ugaki's force pitted the men of the *Musashi* against those of the *Yamato*. Force A, of which the *Yamato* was the flagship, would attack the anchorage, which would be defended by Force B, with the *Musashi* as the leader of the defense. Then their positions would be reversed. This sort of training went on night after night, as the fleet practiced night maneuvers.

Equipped with radar, the Japanese felt that their proficiency in night fighting might bring them the edge in the fall battle that they sought. They expected the decisive battle to be fought at night, for they knew very well that the enemy had control of the skies during the daylight hours. They were also concerned about enemy submarine activity, so they spent much time on anti-submarine defenses.[12]

Admiral Ugaki was as eager for the decisive battle as anyone, but he had one cardinal principle that he enunciated to his chief of staff and the other members of his staff: He would not take the *Yamato* and the *Musashi* into a suicidal situation if he could help it.

In September the fleet continued to train and to wait. The maneuvers of the American fleet around the Philippines indicated that the battle would be fought there. The feeling was that the enemy's land forces represented their weak point and that it might be possible to beat them and win the decisive victory. By this time the Japanese high command had adopted and rejected several plans. The latest to be adopted was the Sho plan, which meant Operation Victory. The battle might be fought in the Philippines, or in Taiwan, or the Ryukyu Islands, or on Honshu and Kyushu, or on Hokkaido and the Kurile Islands. No one knew where, and everyone was looking over Ugaki's shoulder.[13]

By September 21 Admiral Ugaki believed the battle would be fought in the Philippines. That day more than eight hundred American carrier planes struck targets in the Manila area, destroying many aircraft and wrecking installations at the Clark Field complex, as the Japanese had wrecked them for the Americans just over three years earlier. Next morning the Americans were back with another three hundred planes, raiding again. It certainly looked as though the next American assault against the Empire would be coming to the Philippines.

Yet the decreasing number of Allied planes in the attack and the slackening off of it on the second day indicated to Admiral Ugaki that the attack they expected in the Philippines was not coming just now. He indicated this in a message to Admiral Toyoda, commander of the Combined Fleet, who seemed about to launch the Sho operation prematurely. In the next few days Admiral Halsey's operations around the Philippines and Palau cut a wide swath that left everybody confused as to the timing of the American attack and where it was going to occur.

On October 10 the enemy appeared to be heading for Okinawa and later headed south. What was he up to? It was extremely difficult for Imperial General Headquarters to determine and thus to make any plans to concentrate its air and sea forces. But one fact was now certain: The day of the decisive battle was coming very near, and Admiral Ugaki was ready for it.[14]

_____

The End of Power

On October 10, 1944, planes of Admiral Halsey's U.S. Third Fleet struck Okinawa and the smaller Ryukyu Islands. Admiral Toyoda, commander of the Combined Fleet, happened to be in Taiwan at the time inspecting the Sixth Base Air Force, and his chief of staff, Admiral Kusaka, sent out an alert that morning to the Sixth Base Air Force to be ready for Sho 1, the attack on the Philippines, or Sho 2, the attack on Taiwan itself. Kusaka also ordered the six remaining Japanese aircraft carriers to fly off their planes to land bases for the coming battle, and this was done.[1]

On October 12 Admiral Halsey's Third Fleet carrier aircraft attacked Taiwan where the Japanese naval air forces under Vice Admiral Shigeru Fukudome had assembled to support Operation Sho, no matter which way it went. This unit, the Sixth Base Air Force, was at the time the strongest air force of any outside the Japanese islands themselves. In a series of raids on the Philippines in September and early October, the Americans had blasted the First Air fleet, which was located in the Philippines. In August and September the First Air Fleet, which had been moved from the Marianas when the Americans conquered those islands, had been rebuilt to a strength of more than 500 aircraft. But then the U.S. Third Fleet came in to soften up Japanese air power in the region for the landings on Moritai and Peleliu in the Palau Islands, and ranging around the Philippines had destroyed half the First Air Fleet's planes. In the September raids the Japanese air force was reduced to fewer than 250 planes. The rebuilding process began immediately, because the Japanese faced the possibility of a new invasion at any minute, and many planes were sent down from Japan. Bad weather and the lack of experience of new pilots in flying over vast stretches of sea took a high toll, and most of the planes did not arrive.[2]

On October 13 planes of the special Japanese naval attack force called the T Force searched vainly for the American fleet in the Okinawa area, but the weather prevented them from finding the enemy. That night, however, Japanese planes from the Philippines attacked again at twilight. One of them, piloted by Rear Admiral Masufuni Arima, attempted to crash into the carrier *Franklin* and managed to hit the flight deck, slithered across it and burst into flames, and fell overboard, doing some minor damage. It had been Admiral Arima's intent to crash into a carrier, and in this sense he was the first kamikaze. That same day the heavy cruiser *Canberra* was hit by a torpedo. On October 15 Halsey's fleet again attacked Taiwan and northern Luzon, and on October 16 Admiral Toyoda ordered the three Japanese striking forces that would participate in Operation Sho to be prepared to move on short notice.

On October 17 the advance force of the U.S. Seventh Fleet landed on Suluan Island at the mouth of Leyte Gulf. The small Japanese garrison there was able to alert Manila and then was overwhelmed and their radio went silent.

As soon as that landing was verified at Imperial General Headquarters in Tokyo, Admiral Toyoda issued the orders to begin Operation Sho 1, which meant the Philippines; the obvious landing place of the Americans was going to be Leyte Island. The aerial aspect of the operation was entrusted to the

Sixth Base Air Force on Taiwan and the First Air Fleet in the Philippines. But as the operation got under way, neither Japanese air unit was in any condition to perform well because of all the previous raids by Halsey's fleet on Taiwan and the Philippines. The Fifth Base Air Force in the Philippines at this point consisted of only 150 operational aircraft plus whatever the army had to offer, which was unknown to the navy. But as bad as the situation was, it was made worse by the attitude of Vice Admiral Kimpei Teraoka, who seemed to Admiral Toyoda (who had recently made a trip to the Philippines) to be completely dispirited. So Admiral Toyoda appointed Vice Admiral Takejiro Ohnishi to command the Fifth Base Air Force, and he arrived to replace Teraoka on October 17.[3]

For some months Admiral Ohnishi had been advocating the establishment of a new sort of Japanese air force. Now that the carriers were mostly gone, and the best of the carrier pilots as well, drastic measures were needed if the navy was to perform. Ohnishi's solution was the establishment of a suicide air force composed of volunteers who wanted to give their all for the Emperor and the country. They would be sent on one-way attack missions, their aircraft loaded with explosives so that they became flying bombs, and their task would be to crash into a ship, preferably a carrier. If the American carriers could be removed from the scene, the Japanese surface fleet had every confidence in its ability to defeat the American surface fleet in a decisive engagement. But another one of Admiral Ohnishi's demands made it more difficult for the Japanese surface fleet, and particularly Admiral Ugaki's battle squadron, to succeed in its mission. Since the Japanese scouting force in the Philippines had been decimated and there were not enough aircraft with long enough range to fly scouting missions to find the enemy forces, all the seaplanes of the battleships and cruisers were transferred to San Jose on the island of Mindoro. Thus, when Admiral Ugaki prepared to sail on his mission to destroy the American landings on Leyte, he was deprived of his eyes, the observation planes that his battleships had carried. As one officer of the battle squadron remarked when he heard of the order, "I'd hate to be responsible for this decision when the enemy submarines attack."[4]

It was 11 o'clock in the morning of October 18 when the order to execute the Sho plan was received by Admiral Takeo Kurita and passed to Admiral Ugaki and the other unit commanders. One unit, led by Vice Admiral Teiji Nishimura, would move down south, through Surigao Strait, and then turn to attack the Leyte invasion fleet from the south. It would be followed by another force led by Vice Admiral Kiyohide Shima. The main force, which was commanded by Admiral Kurita himself and which included Ugaki's battleships, would go through San Bernardino Strait, north of Leyte, and come down from the north to meet the Nishimura and Shima forces and make a pincers movement on the American ships at Leyte. Meanwhile Admiral Ozawa would take his aircraft carriers down from Japan to the waters off Luzon Island, and there he would distract Admiral Halsey's Third Fleet so the Japanese surface ships could succeed in their mission of destroying the American invasion fleet and stopping the invasion.

But in spite of all the months of fleet training in night fighting, the high command suddenly ordered the fleet to move into Leyte Gulf in the daylight hours of October 25. The officers and men were stunned by this turn of events, and morale was badly damaged before they set out on the mission.[5]

Admiral Ugaki's ships weighed anchor at 1 o'clock in the morning of October 18 and arrived at the assembly point in Brunei at noon on October 20. There the fleet fueled. They were supposed to leave again at 8 o'clock on the morning of October 22.

But now many officers began to learn that the Americans had landed on Leyte on October 17 and that most of the ships had already unloaded and left for ports of resupply. What they would find at Leyte Gulf would be supply ships and auxiliaries. If they sank them all they would not seriously affect the course of the battle ashore, for the troops ashore had already moved inland and broken the first line of Japanese army defenses. The best that the attacks on Leyte could bring was a short surcease in the Allied campaign.

So what was the use of it? The navy senior officers were prepared to sacrifice their lives and their ships if necessary for the good of the Empire, but many of them objected to what they saw as waste from the beginning. The complaint grew so serious that Admiral Kurita decided he had to deal with it. On the evening of October 21 he called to the flagship, the cruiser *Atago*, the division commanders, and their staff officers. When they had assembled and quieted down, Admiral Kurita spoke.

I know that many of you are strongly opposed to this assignment. But the war situation is far more critical than any of you can possibly know. Would it not be a shame to have the fleet remaining intact while our nation perishes? I believe that Imperial General Headquarters is giving us a glorious opportunity. Because I realize how very serious the war situation actually is, I am willing to accept even this ultimate assignment to storm into Leyte Gulf.

You must all remember that there are such things as miracles. What man can say that there is no chance for our fleet to turn the tide of war in a decisive battle? We shall have a chance to meet our enemies. We shall engage his task forces. I hope that you will not carry your responsibilities lightly. I know that you will act faithfully and well.

As the admiral concluded, his officers all stood and cheered, "Banzai! Banzai! Banzai!"[6]

But some of them still left the room filled with foreboding that the mission was designed to fail.

Anyone who saw the Japanese Second Fleet moving out of Brunei Bay on the morning of October 22 had to be impressed, and some of the officers and men convinced themselves that they had a chance of victory. Their force was formidable.

First were the two huge battleships of Admiral Ugaki's Battleship Division One, the *Yamato* and the *Musashi* with their 18-inch guns, and the *Nagato* with its 16-inch guns. They were followed by the older battleships *Kongo* and *Haruna*. Then there were the cruisers, three divisions of them, the *Atago, Takao, Maya, Chokai, Myoko, Haguro, Kumano, Suzuya, Tone,* and *Chikuma*; and then the light cruisers *Yahagi* and *Noshiro* and fifteen destroyers. Of course there were no carriers. But the plan called for the Japanese naval air force of the Philippines to protect the ships in their passage through these waters by the use of land-based aircraft. The men of the Second Fleet did not know that Japanese naval air power in the Philippines had all but disappeared and that what was left of it was not being used to escort surface ships but to mount attacks on the enemy fleet.

The Japanese Second Fleet split into two sections and steamed north toward the Suluan Sea at 18 knots, zigzagging to avoid enemy submarines. On the second morning, in the narrow waters of Palawan Passage, they ran afoul of two American submarines, the *Darter* and the *Dace*. The submarines sank the fleet flagship, the cruiser *Atago*, and put two torpedoes into the *Takao*, which remained afloat but had to return to the Brunei base and remained out of action. They also sank the cruiser *Maya*, which blew up.

In the confusion Admiral Ugaki assumed command of the Japanese Second Fleet and supervised the hunt for the Allied submarines, but he did not have command for long. After a short swim, Admiral Kurita and his staff were picked up by a destroyer after their flagship sank. They were delivered to the *Yamato*, where Kurita reasserted command.

The Japanese Second Fleet moved steadily toward its objective. The morning of October 24 dawned bright and clear. Just after 8 o'clock in the morning, as the Japanese fleet was

rounding the southern tip of Mindoro Island and entering
Tablas Strait, the lookouts aboard the *Yamato* sighted an
American carrier plane. A few minutes later Admiral Halsey
had a report from the plane about the Japanese fleet, and he
ordered the carriers to send attack forces after the Japanese
ships.[7]

When the Japanese fleet reached Coron Bay, a tanker came
out and fueled the destroyers. Soon the force was through the
Tablas Strait and into the Sibuyan Sea. At about 10:30 A.M.
the Second Fleet began to come under air attack from the
American carriers. The Japanese ships opened up with their
anti-aircraft guns, but the firing was not very accurate. The
American planes were aggressive and there were many of
them. Between 10:30 A.M. and the coming of twilight, more
than 250 planes attacked the Japanese Second Fleet. "The small
number of enemy planes shot down is regrettable," Admiral
Ugaki wrote in his diary that night.[8]

That day Admiral Ugaki had very little time to write. In
the first air strike, the Americans concentrated on the battleship *Musashi*, and she was hit by one bomb and one torpedo.
She could still make 27 knots. But in the next two hours the
Musashi was hit by four more torpedoes and four more
bombs. She began to lose power and fell astern of the other
battleships. Her speed was cut to 22 knots.

Admiral Kurita reduced the fleet speed, but the *Musashi*
began to fall behind. Admiral Kurita sent a message to
Imperial Headquarters and the Fifth Base Air Force requesting land-based air forces and the carrier force to make
prompt attack on the American carrier force, which was in
Lamon Bay. Kurita had no way of knowing that the land-
based air forces had now been reduced to fewer than one
hundred planes. The Ozawa carriers had landed most of their
planes to fight the battle of Formosa, and they had been lost
in the battle. So no air support was forthcoming.

By 1:30 in the afternoon the *Musashi* was 10 miles back,
obviously a cripple. The planes from the next air strike of the

American carriers concentrated on her then. By 3 o'clock in the afternoon she had been hit by nineteen torpedoes and seventeen bombs. Her speed was reduced to 12 knots. She was taking water and was in danger of sinking, so Admiral Ugaki ordered her commander, Rear Admiral Toshiro Inoguchi, to beach the ship. The commander tried, but by that time her entire system had broken down and she was flooding fast.

As darkness began to fall she was listing 30 degrees, and two destroyers were standing by her. At 7:30 P.M. the captain ordered the ship abandoned, and five minutes later she capsized and sank, taking down 39 officers and 984 men. But more than 80 officers and more than 1,300 men were rescued by destroyers and taken to Manila.[9]

Admiral Ugaki fought the rest of the battle aboard the *Yamato*, with almost half his division lost. That battleship and the *Nagato* were both hit by bombs, but their fighting ability was not seriously diminished. The other damage to the Second Fleet this day was to the heavy cruiser *Myoko*, which was hit by a torpedo. It caused enough damage to make her return to Brunei Bay. But the rest of the Second Fleet went on, heading for San Bernardino Strait and the northern passage that would take them down on Leyte Gulf the following morning. The Japanese fleet was still powerful enough: four battleships, six cruisers, two light cruisers, and a dozen destroyers. The real trouble was the absence of any air support, which made the fleet sitting ducks for American airmen.

As the Japanese Second Fleet continued on toward San Bernardino Strait, Admiral Kurita took stock. The *Yamato* was in good fighting trim, but the *Nagato* had been slowed to 20 knots by two torpedo hits. The light cruiser *Yahagi* was damaged so that she could only make 22 knots. Several other ships had suffered damages. Admiral Kurita reduced the fleet speed to 18 knots, and some of his officers wondered how he expected to get through San Bernardino Strait and make an attack the next day.

At 3:55 in the afternoon as the ships were about to enter

the narrow part of the San Bernardino passage, Kurita suddenly ordered the ships to reverse course. He told Admiral Toyoda why in a message. "As a result of five aerial attacks from 6:30 until 3:30 our damages are not light. The frequency and numerical strength of these enemy attacks is increasing. If we continue our present course our losses will increase incalculably, with little hope of success for our mission." (His intelligence officers estimated that the American carriers could launch at least three more attacks on the Second Fleet before darkness came in.) "Therefore," he said, "I have decided to withdraw outside the range of enemy air attack for the time being, and to resume our sortie in coordination with successful attacks on the enemy by our air forces."[10]

Was this message sent tongue in cheek? Perhaps it was, although such was not common within the Imperial Navy. In any event Admiral Kurita was trying to tell Admiral Toyoda that he really needed air support if the attack on Leyte Gulf was going to meet with success. But of course there was nothing Toyoda could do, because there was no air support available anywhere.

So Admiral Kurita broke off the attack and the *Yamato* and the other ships headed back into the Sibuyan Sea. Admiral Kurita sailed back toward Brunei for a few hours, then turned about again and headed for San Bernardino Strait. He had not received any reply to his call for land-based aircraft support, but neither had the fleet been attacked again (as he had expected it would), so he was ready to make the attempt once more. He hoped to get through the strait in the night-time hours and arrive on the Leyte side at daybreak. He hoped for land-based air attacks on the carriers that he expected to find there.

The Japanese Second Fleet came out of San Bernardino Strait at dawn on October 25. There was not a ship or a plane in sight. As far as Admiral Kurita and Admiral Ugaki could see, the ocean ahead was clear.

What had happened was that two parts of the Sho plan had

to this point worked almost to perfection. The plan called for Kurita to go through San Bernardino Strait while the American carrier fleet was being lured north by Ozawa's carrier fleet. So far so good; both aims had been accomplished. Although Kurita's fleet had been hit hard with the loss of a battleship, the sinking of two cruisers, and the disablement of two more, it was still a strong fighting force. But the parts of the plan that had miscarried were the attacks by Admiral Nishimura and Admiral Shima through the Surigao Strait and the support of the land-based aircraft, which were supposed to protect all these naval units. Nishimura had run into disaster in Surigao Strait; he had been harried all the way through the Sea of Mindanao by planes and PT boats, and finally he had been attacked by destroyers. Almost his entire force had been lost, and Nishimura himself had died in the battle. Admiral Shima, coming up behind him, had seen the remnants of Nishimura's force burning on the water and had turned about and headed away from Surigao Strait. In so doing he had saved part of his force.

As for the land-based air forces, they had exhausted their force in early morning attacks on the American carrier fleet that lay to the east of Leyte; they lost most of their planes. Throughout the rest of the action in the Philippines, they were reduced to kamikaze suicide action, not having enough planes to mount any sort of counteroffensive.[11]

When the Japanese Second Fleet moved out of San Bernardino Strait and headed south along the shore of Samar Island toward Leyte Gulf on the morning of October 25, the force interposed between the attacking Japanese and the supply ships standing off Leyte consisted almost entirely of escort carriers and destroyers and destroyer escorts, but the Japanese did not know this. They came out of the strait and when the sun rose just before 6:30 they were moving south, puzzled by not being attacked. They were shifting into circular formation against air attack at 6:45 when suddenly four ships were sighted on the horizon to the southeast; they were seen to be launching aircraft. Here at last was the enemy carrier fleet, said the Japanese, for which they had been waiting since Midway. Admiral Kurita radioed to Tokyo: "Here by heaven-sent opportunity, we are dashing to attack the enemy carriers. Our first objective is to destroy the flight decks, then the task force."[12]

So Admiral Kurita ordered full speed ahead on an attack course bound directly for the enemy. The fleet speeded up from 18 knots. The 18-inch guns of the *Yamato* fired a full salvo of shells at 6:59 A.M., and the mast top lookout reported a hit. It was on the escort carrier *Gambier Bay*. (The report was incorrect; the *Gambier Bay* was sunk by shells from the battleship *Kongo*.) In a short time the ship had broken in two and sunk.

During the next hour the American ships began to attack on their own, and the Japanese thought they were facing cruisers, so vigorous were the attacks of the destroyers and destroyer escorts in launching torpedoes and firing with their guns. In this battle Admiral Ugaki was little but a spectator, because Admiral Kurita directed the fighting himself and the safety of the *Yamato* (on which both admirals were riding) depended on Rear Admiral Nobuei Morishita, the captain of the ship.

The American planes from the carriers began to attack the Japanese ships and did serious damage to the cruisers *Chikuma* and *Chokai*, which were forced out of the fight and assigned destroyers for protection. For two hours the battle raged. The American plane attacks became better coordinated and seemed to be coming in waves. Just after 9 o'clock that morning Admiral Kurita turned his ships resolutely toward Leyte and broke off the pursuit of the American carriers. In the fight the Americans had lost the *Gambier Bay* carrier, two destroyers, and one destroyer escort. The Japanese lost the heavy cruisers *Chikuma*, *Chokai*, and *Suzuya*, as well as three destroyers. The fight was a victory for the Americans, although no one knew it at the time.

When Kurita broke off the pursuit of the American ships

and headed into Leyte Gulf, the fleet was scattered over an area of 22 miles. It took two hours to form up for the Leyte Gulf attack, and it was almost 11:30 A.M. when the Japanese headed for Leyte Gulf. At the time of the sailing from Brunei Bay on October 22, the fleet had consisted of thirty-two vessels. It was now down to fifteen ships, but Kurita seemed determined to carry out his mission. At noon on October 25 he radioed to Tokyo: "We are determined to execute the planned penetration of Leyte Gulf despite any enemy air attacks that may be encountered."[13]

At this point the Japanese Second Fleet was about 45 miles from the Leyte beaches. This meant that in two hours Kurita could be using the big guns of the battleships to destroy the transports and, he hoped, to cripple the invasion army that was now on the beaches and in the interior of Leyte Island.

But in the course of the battle Kurita had been getting messages in the clear, sent by various American ships calling for help, and the answer had been from the Seventh Fleet that help was two hours away from the escort carriers. This meant that if Kurita continued his attack in two hours, what he must consider to be a superior force would be approaching him. His ships would all be at risk because they had no air cover of any kind. The same was true if he continued the charges into Leyte Gulf, where he expected to meet nothing but empty cargo ships and transports. To sacrifice the Japanese fleet for a handful of empty cargo vessels seemed foolish, and when he had a report of an enemy task force north of Suluan Island, he decided to turn to that force and battle there instead. So the Japanese Second Fleet turned away from the Leyte beaches, heading northward to find the American task force and engage it in final battle. In such a battle the power of the *Yamato* would be immense. Thus far in the war she had expended only 81 of the 1,100 shells for her main 18-inch batteries. A single 18-inch shell was enough to sink a carrier. So the ships of Kurita's force headed into what they thought would be a battle with naval forces.

Shortly after 1 o'clock in the afternoon they came under attack by a wave of American planes, then two more waves followed within two hours. It was estimated that the enemy was northeast of Kurita's force. There was no way of checking exactly, because Kurita had no planes to send aloft and the enemy was out of range of the Second Fleet. None of the attacks were as skillfully pursued as those of the morning and the previous days had been. After the third attack, however, matters of time and space and fuel began to be major concerns.[14]

At 4 o'clock in the afternoon, for the first time since the expedition had set out, air support appeared. A flight of some sixty Japanese aircraft appeared in the sky and requested information about the enemy ships, which Kurita could not supply. The air armada flew away and later reappeared, saying they could not find the enemy.

If they could not find the enemy, then how could Kurita find them? Admiral Kurita pondered the problem. He did not have much time. Some sort of decision had to be made, and he had already decided against wasting the fleet on an empty victory over some transports off Leyte. That would accomplish nothing to shorten the war.

So Admiral Kurita turned back to San Bernardino Strait, went through the strait that night, and headed toward the anchorage at Brunei without attacking the ships off Leyte. Once again the great battleship *Yamato* had been within a narrow margin of engagement in a major sea battle, and once again the opportunity had slipped away. That night Kurita sent messages to Admiral Ohnishi and Admiral Fukudome, commanders of the land-based air forces fighting in the Philippines, asking them to strike the enemy who most certainly would be attacking Kurita the next day.

As if on a schedule, the Americans came the following day. On October 26 they hit the Japanese fleet as it was moving through the Sibuyan Sea on the way to Brunei. The cruiser *Noshiro* was disabled by a torpedo, and the *Yamato* took bombs from the carrier planes. Then, at 10:49 in the morning, thirty B-24 bombers found the fleet and bombed the *Yamato* almost exclusively. One bomb flooded her anchor room, and another opened a hole in the side at the waterline abreast of the forward main turret. A third wave of carrier planes sank the *Noshiro* and hit the *Yamato* again with three bombs. Several near misses did other damage to the big battleship. Other planes found the *Nagato* and scored four direct hits and nine near misses on her.

The fleet staggered homeward, most of the ships now leaking oil and taking on water from loosened rivets and seams. In traversing the dangerous ground near Palawan, Admiral Kurita deliberately chose a path through the shallows. Here, in the narrow channels surrounded by rocks and shoals, the enemy's submarines would find it difficult to operate. By so doing Kurita avoided new submarine attacks and arrived at Brunei Bay without further incident on October 28. Of all his ships only one destroyer had come through the battle without any damage at all.

As for Admiral Ugaki, the outcome of the battle made his command quite meaningless. As never before he recognized the change in the tactics and strategy of naval battle. The days of the battleship as a major factor in decisive naval action had definitely ended. The battleship *Yamato*, pride of the Japanese fleet, had become a useless anomaly. It was enormously powerful but completely unable to come to grips with the realities of the new sort of naval battle.

Admiral Ugaki was exhausted emotionally and sick physically from the strain. He and Kurita and the others had gone into this venture prepared to sacrifice their lives in the service of the Emperor to stop the American drive on Leyte. They had failed. Their naval world was in tatters. Ugaki thought about committing ritual suicide because of the failure. But the war was not yet over. Perhaps he would have a new opportunity to serve his Emperor and strike a blow for Japan when he died. There was time enough to consider *seppuku* when the war was lost.

_____

The Fifth Air Fleet

Admiral Ugaki was relieved of command of the First Battleship Division that fall. What was left of the fleet was reorganized and the *Yamato* was brought back to Japan. Admiral Ugaki was recalled to the Navy Ministry. When he got there, still pale and suffering from the effects of many months on the battlefront, he found that there was plenty of sympathy for him but no employment. He went from one bureau to another and it was always the same. The navy was shrinking, not growing, and the market for vice admirals was extremely limited. He was told to go on leave; they would call him when they needed him.

He took the opportunity while he was at the Navy Ministry to look at his personal file. He was upset to discover that the navy had followed its old policies and that he and all the others connected with the Second Fleet's failed mission at Leyte Gulf had been held responsible for the failure. The fact that he had been wounded in the action did not mean anything in terms of the personnel record.[1]

He had not recovered from this disappointment when in Tokyo one day he was subjected to one of the early B-29 air raids, which was a real shock. In fact, it shocked Admiral Ugaki out of growing lethargy and restored his fighting spirit, a fact that he managed to communicate to the powers of the Navy Ministry and the Naval High Command.

There was nothing Ugaki could do about the B-29 bombers. This was an army problem, and the army had taken over the responsibility for combating them. New, longer range anti-aircraft guns were being built, as well as new fighter planes that would be able to move up to 30,000 feet where the B-29s operated, 5,000 feet above the maximum range of the current fighters. The army had no intention of sharing this responsibility with the navy, but the navy had other equally important responsibilities to pursue.

Therefore, on February 2, 1945, Ugaki was called to come to a meeting, but not at the ministry. This meeting was to be held at the navy minister's house, and a commander came to escort the admiral, his mysterious bearing indicating that something unusual and important was afoot.

When Admiral Ugaki got to the minister's house, he found that most of the Naval High Command was assembled there. Almost straightaway they offered him a new job. It would be to undertake the defense of Kyushu, one of the two main home islands, and the defense of the southwestern sea approaches and of Okinawa. It was not going to be an easy job. It would demand the same sort of sacrifice that he and Admiral Kurita had attempted to make in Operation Sho. But this time he would be overseeing an entire suicide air force, for that was the route the Japanese navy had decided to take.

The First Air Fleet had been moved to Taiwan from the Philippines after the American invasion of Luzon Island and the march toward Manila, and it would remain there with its three hundred aircraft for the defense of that island. The Third Air Fleet, with about eight hundred aircraft, was commanded by Vice Admiral Teraoka, who at the moment was still resisting the kamikaze idea. He had to be converted and made to take on new responsibility, but he would remain in charge of the defense of Honshu, one of the two main islands of Japan. Admiral Ugaki was offered an equally important command—one that was more important at the moment, command of the forces that would battle against the Allies in the open sea off the Japanese shores. Specifically, they expected attacks on Iwo Jima, about which not much could be done, and on Okinawa, about which everything had to be done to slow down the Allied advance.

Imperial General Headquarters was still trying to put together a cogent policy, but the navy had decided that since it had no ships, it must adopt the suicide principle for all its operations. Thus, the submarine force was concentrating on the building of *kaiten*, midget suicide submarines, and the construction of suicide motor boats. A new sort of aircraft was in the testing stage—the Oka, or flying bomb—which would be added to the navy arsenal. The navy aviation schools would be converted to training pilots for kamikaze missions. A few units would be maintained at the old level, mostly of the more experienced pilots. They would be expected to help in the training, and one of their principal jobs would be to escort suicide missions, watch them, and come home to report on their successes and failures.

All this was laid out for Admiral Ugaki that evening. Then he was asked if he would take command of the Fifth Air Fleet, to rebuild it as an integral part of the defense of Japan.

It was made clear that the fortunes of the nation are in the hands of the Imperial Navy. I have been offered in effect the key to the gate of the Imperial fortunes. It is certainly all life and death struggle. In such a crisis there was but one action to take. I had to accept. Surely in the crises of this life or death struggle the end cannot be conquest.[2]

After Ugaki had accepted the new assignments, he was congratulated and asked to stay at the ministry for dinner. So that night as the highest officials of the navy met and discussed their perilous affairs, Admiral Ugaki listened.

His first order of business would be to organize the Fifth Air Fleet for the defense of the south. His second assignment, he learned that night, would be to prepare the Fifth Air Fleet for a major undertaking, a mission against the Allied base at Ulithi in the western Caroline Island group, which the Americans had made into their forward fleet base for the Philippine operations and had been using ever since. This is where the Allied aircraft carriers went to replenish their stores and ammunition. This is where the greatest concentration of carriers could be found at the proper times. If the Japanese were lucky enough to choose a propitious moment for attack, they might wipe out most of the strength of the American carrier fleet, and then the Allies would have to call a halt, temporarily at least, to the campaign that was coming ever closer to Japan. In the halt period, it might be possible to secure the sort of concessions from the Allies that the Imperial Army generals demanded as the price of ending the war.

The mission against the Ulithi base was to be called the Tan Mission. A select group of pilots would be brought together and sent off in twin-engine aircraft, the only sort that had the range to make such a long mission. There would not be enough fuel to get them there and back again. That meant the deliberate sacrifice of an entire air group, but there was nothing to be done about it. Japan had lost all the intermediate bases such as the Philippines that once could have been refueling points. Now Japan was about to lose Iwo Jima, or so it seemed from the level of activity around that volcanic island.

Admiral Ugaki left the minister's official residence with his head full of new ideas, and he prepared to go to Kyushu and establish himself at Kanoya air base on the southern tip of that island. Its warm climate would be welcome in this wintery February, for palm trees grew in southern Kyushu and the climate was tamed by soft currents from the south. But Kanoya was located in a remote area, so deserted a countryside that the major barracks for the pilots would have to be a disused middle school. As for the rest, the existing air base would have to be enlarged and some of the elements built into the hillside for safety against marauding Allied aircraft.

In a few days, Ugaki had made his first trip to Kanoya.

"Everything about it is good but the fact that in the field family life suffers. I have to be prepared at any moment for duty."

But to Admiral Ugaki in the winter of 1945 this was no great sacrifice. His wife had died more than three years earlier, and his children kept the house in Tokyo. He had been there so little since the beginning of the Pacific phase of the war that he was not missed. His life in Kyushu would be the life of the soldier, and that suited him very well, for his whole being was wrapped up in the prosecution of the war on behalf of Emperor and nation.

From now on he was to be responsible for all operations in the south, but at the moment there was one matter in the works. If the American fleet appeared, it must be fought off. And until Admiral Ugaki had a chance to organize his Fifth Fleet, that would be the task of the existing organization, the Third Air Fleet on Honshu Island.[3]

On February 13 Admiral Ugaki was taking the train back from Kyushu when he encountered Admiral Teraoka. They had not met since the days in the Combined Fleet, so it was a pleasant encounter. More than that, they had the coming Tan Mission to talk about. Since Admiral Teraoka's purview included the training command of the navy, Admiral Ugaki asked him to set up a special training program for the pilots who would be engaged in the Tan Mission. They had to be made thoroughly familiar with twin-engined bomber operations. The sooner they could mount the Tan Mission, the better. Admiral Ugaki had been told that day that the American carrier fleet had just left Ulithi. That meant the Japanese could expect a new strike by that carrier fleet somewhere.

On February 15 Japanese scout planes sighted the American carrier fleet south of Iwo Jima. This was an obvious target for them. As everyone knew, the Americans would be wanting bases for their fighter aircraft to accompany the B-29s based in the Marianas. Iwo Jima seemed a logical choice. An attack there was expected momentarily.

But that was not what was on the minds of the Americans

at the moment. The attack on Iwo Jima did not materialize. Instead, at dawn on February 16, eleven American fleet carriers and five light carriers moved to within 60 miles of the Honshu coast and at dawn launched their first air strikes. The attack came as a complete surprise to the Third Air Fleet, and Admiral Teraoka managed to get his planes into the air barely in time to challenge the enemy planes as they crossed the coastline. All day long the Americans ranged around Honshu Island, striking airfields near Tokyo. The purpose of the attack was to cut down the number of aircraft the Japanese would have available to send to Iwo Jima, for indeed Iwo Jima was the object of the next Allied invasion.

The American planes attacked the airfields around Tokyo and then hit several aircraft factories as well. Night put an end to the raids, but the Americans were back the next morning, hitting airfields, factories, and shipping around Tokyo. A change in the weather off Tokyo that was much for the worse saved the area from further pounding after lunch on February 17. Admiral Marc Mitscher took his planes back on board and headed at high speed for Iwo Jima, where they were to support the invasion that came on February 19.[4]

Back in Japan, the Imperial Navy was upset about the easy success the Americans had scored in this attack on the homeland. Admiral Teraoka's Third Air Fleet had lost 105 planes, many of them destroyed on the ground, and had been unable to put very many fighters up after the first strikes because the Americans kept hitting their air bases time and again. So preparations were made for a kamikaze attack on the American fleet. Even Teraoka was becoming convinced that this was the only option left for Japan.

The unit chosen to make this strike was the 601st Air Group, which had been training for carrier operations until it became apparent that there would be no more carrier operations. Although this was to be a kamikaze operation, Admiral Teraoka could not bring himself to order such a direct approach and the air crews were instructed to attack as they wished. They could drop their bombs and strafe or they could barrel in to crash. Thirty-two planes took off from Katori air base near Yokosuka and flew to Kanoya on the first leg of their mission. At Kanoya they were met by Admiral Ugaki, who gave them breakfast as their planes were refueled and a pep talk, reminding them of their duty to Emperor and country. Then he brought out special sake that had been a gift from the throne, and the pilots and staff toasted the mission and their coming successes. They had changed the name of their unit for the occasion and were now known as Mitate Unit No. 2. After breakfast the Mitate Unit was on its way to the Bonins for more fuel. Late in the afternoon it found the American carriers northwest of Iwo Jima.

The Americans were not really expecting an attack so soon, and when the first report of a number of "bogies" came in, the planes were identified as friendly because no action was taken. It was not until two of the "friendly" planes tried to attack and were shot down that the air intelligence officers changed their minds.

Two of the carriers in the American fleet were equipped with night fighters. But on this night the task force was moving afield from the amphibious forces, and Admiral Mitscher took the carrier *Enterprise* to provide night cover for the task force. That left the *Saratoga* to give cover to the rest of the fleet. The carrier was about 35 miles northwest of Iwo Jima at 4:30 in the afternoon when the first planes were reported 75 miles away. In all the confusion it was not until twenty minutes later that the planes were identified as enemy, and by that time they were attacking. Six planes of the Mitate Unit No. 2 burst out of the cloud cover above the ships and into the hail of anti-aircraft fire put up by the *Saratoga* and her supporting ships. Two of them were shot down and bounced from the surface of the water into the side of the *Saratoga* at the waterline. Their bombs were thrown into the inside of the ship, where they exploded. The *Saratoga* had just completed launching fifteen planes when she was hit, and two fighters were still in the catapults when she was hit again by a bomb from a third plane that did not choose to crash. The bomb exploded on the anchor windlass, which put much of the flight deck in the forward part of the ship out of action. A fourth plane was shot down without doing any harm to the ship, but the fifth crashed into the port catapult and exploded. The sixth plane crashed into a crane on the starboard side of the ship and parts of it landed in the gun galleries along the edge of the flight deck.

The entire attack was over in three minutes, and the skies and sea were quiet except for smoke from the anti-aircraft guns and the burning Japanese planes and the fires they had started.

Saratoga was hurt as a carrier, but as a ship she built up a speed of 25 knots while fighting fires. She was soon jettisoning the burning aircraft and bringing her fires under control.

All this was well along by 6:45 P.M., but then the men of the ship saw a number of parachute flares light up and five more Japanese planes attacked the *Saratoga*. Four of them were shot down without doing any harm, but the fifth got inside the anti-aircraft screen unobserved and dropped a bomb that exploded just over the flight deck, blowing a 25-foot-square hole in that deck. Still, three hours later the *Saratoga* was recovering aircraft on the after part of her flight deck. She steamed under her own power to Eniwetok and then to the west coast for repairs. She had lost forty-two planes either by direct attack or by water landings because they could not land on the carrier, and she had casualties of 123 killed and 192 wounded. She would be out of action in the Pacific for the next three months.[5]

As the second attack came in on the *Saratoga*, other ships also felt the effects of the Mitate Unit's trained fliers. The escort carrier *Bismarck Sea* was about 45 miles east of Iwo Jima when she was hit. Two planes attacked her. One was shot down, but the second came in very low under the anti-aircraft fire. It was 1,000 yards away when it was spotted, but it was too low for the guns to depress properly; it crashed into the ship near the elevator aft and then dropped onto the hangar deck. The bomb exploded. That started gasoline fires on the hangar deck of the *Bismarck Sea*, which then started fires in the torpedo and bomb stowage. More explosions blew out the after end of the hangar deck, and at a little after 7 o'clock that night the captain ordered the ship abandoned. The ship burned and exploded for another three hours, then capsized and sank. Of the crew of 943, 218 officers and men were lost. The rest were picked up by destroyers and destroyer escorts, which spent all night and part of the next morning searching the sea.

Other Japanese planes came in on the escort carrier *Lunga Point*. One launched a torpedo but was splashed and the torpedo missed. A second plane did the same and missed, and the plane flew away safely. A third plane launched a torpedo that also missed, but then the plane hit the island with its wing, skidded across the flight deck, and plunged into the sea after damaging the flight deck. A fourth plane was shot down. The damage to the *Lunga Point* was not serious and no men were killed.

Planes of the Mitate Unit also hit the cargo ship *Keokuk* southeast of Iwo Jima. One hit on the starboard side of the bridge and wiped out all but one 20-millimeter anti-aircraft gun of the starboard battery. Seventeen men were killed and 44 wounded. Finally, the *LST 477* was hit by a kamikaze, which bounced overboard without doing much damage but thoroughly frightened the crew.

So the thirty-two planes of Mitate Unit No. 2 scored very well for themselves: Nineteen of them had managed to attack ships of the American fleet, sinking one small carrier, damaging another and a cargo ship, and doing so much damage to a fleet carrier that it was out of action for three months. If this sort of record could be achieved by every unit, then there was indeed hope for the Japanese plan of causing so much damage to the American carrier fleet that operations would become impossible.[6]

But militating against the Japanese plan was the fact that the Mitate Unit was an anomaly. Not really a kamikaze unit as such, it was composed of a group of fliers who had been training for months for normal carrier work and who were sent on a desperate mission because there was no carrier employment for them any more. The Japanese would look for success from the spirit of the volunteer kamikaze pilots and later from the desperation of those who had been assigned to the suicidal task from which they could not escape. At the moment, the success of the Mitate Unit brought banzais in Tokyo and a fierce desire at Kanoya air base that the planes of the Fifth Air Fleet might do as well.

At Kanoya, Admiral Ugaki made note of the success of the Mitate Unit without comment. There was no follow-up by the Japanese because they had no other unit that was ready for action. And Admiral Ugaki's attention at the moment was focused on the Tan Mission, in which Imperial General Headquarters had so much confidence and so much hope.

The Hope That Failed

At the end of February 1945, Admiral Ugaki was busy planning the Tan Mission according to orders from Imperial General Headquarters. He had discussed the matter with Admiral Teraoka, who ran the training command as well as the Third Air Fleet operations, and the admiral had undertaken the training of some pilots for the Tan force.[1]

The decision had been made early on that they would use the Betty two-engined bomber because of its long range, but the admiral and the high command worried about the nature of the weapon they should deliver. Finally they settled on 800-kilogram (1,760-pound) bombs. Each aircraft could carry only one of these bombs; but one should be enough to sink a carrier, and the plan called for three planes to attack each of eight carriers they expected to find in the anchorage. That meant twenty-four bombers. To that force were added another five flying boats, which would go ahead as an advance unit to report on weather and the Allied defenses and would stay around the fringes of the attack to bring back the news of success.[2]

On February 10 the Tan Mission began with Admiral Toyoda's order to the submarine command, the Sixth Fleet, to send an I-boat escort to the Ulithi base. Already the Fourth

Fleet, still at Truk, was scouting the area aerially. But where were the American carriers?

At the end of the first week of March the Americans had occupied the airfields of Iwo Jima, which meant they could bring in fighters and bombers to be based on the airfields. This, in turn, released the carriers from air duty around the island. Where had they gone? This was important, because the Tan Mission had been scheduled for March 10 as attack day. But reports on March 7 said that the carriers had not come back to Ulithi as they were expected to do.

The Japanese were too impatient. The carriers had indeed returned to Ulithi, where they arrived on March 9, and were reported by a scout plane from Truk. The plane reported five fleet carriers, three light carriers, seven escort carriers, and many other warships, and the pilot reported that as he left the area he had caught a glimpse of another group of four carriers entering the lagoon.[3]

That message was flashed to Tokyo, and from there the orders were given to Admiral Ugaki at Kanoya air base. The raid was on for the morning of March 10.

The pilots and air crews of the Azuza Special Attack Unit, as this force had been named, were all assembled at Kanoya air base. Admiral Ugaki had been giving much thought to his new command and the psychological aspects of the new war he was beginning to fight. He understood very well the philosophy of his airmen and their sensitivity. One of his major tasks, he knew, was to instill in the airmen a determination to succeed in their sacrifice for Emperor and country. It so happened that Admiral Yokoi, his chief of staff, was a lover of fugu, the Japanese blowfish delicacy that is so prized and so difficult to prepare because the blowfish liver is deadly poison and must be carefully removed before cooking.[4]

Ugaki and Admiral Yokoi laid on a special fugu dinner for the young men with plenty of sake, something they were not likely to see elsewhere in Japan. It was all in honor of their coming sacrifice. At the dinner they were toasted and honored and made to feel like living gods. That was the point, to bring them to a state of exhilaration that would carry them through to the end of their lonely trail.

As Admiral Ugaki explained in his diary, the object was to "accelerate the new spirit of the junior officers"—not just the men who would make the sacrifice the next day, but all those who would stay behind and make their sacrifice later. Admiral Ugaki was engaged in changing the psychology of his command, and he was very conscious of the importance of this factor. It could mean the difference between success and failure in the entire kamikaze program.[5]

At 3:30 in the morning the first of the four flying boats set out on its advance mission to go ahead and report the weather for the others all the way to Ulithi. At 4:30 in the morning the other three Kawanishi flying boats were to set out on their forward patrol. One had engine trouble, which delayed the entire operation. An hour and fifteen minutes later, Admiral Ugaki was at his desk and there he found a special message from Admiral Toyoda for the fliers of the Azuza Special Attack Unit. Their training period had not been long, but these were all skilled fliers and volunteers who knew the nature of their one-way missions. They were getting ready, finishing breakfast, adjusting their uniforms and their *hachimakis*—headbands that symbolized the sacrifice they were about to make for Emperor and country. Admiral Ugaki went to meet them and the ceremonial sake was brought out. Ugaki had the message from Admiral Toyoda that was to bring a new era to Japanese naval affairs. It had been prepared with great care:

By order of the commander of the Combined Fleet, based on authoritative reports, the Azuza Special Attack Unit will sortie today as according to previous instructions.

The war situation grows daily more perilous as the enemy B-29 bombers raid the homeland.

The enemy carrier force has twice struck the Kanto Plain without our being able to stop them.

On Iwo Jima our comrades at arms are engaged in a deadly

battle, day and night, under conditions that indicate they will fight to the death.

The Empire will survive or fall through the success or failure of this endeavor against the American fleet.

Let all members of the Special Attack Unit give their utmost and do their best to annihilate the enemy, the leaders to direct the unit to success, and the subordinates to do their best.

You are first in our hearts as we bid farewell to you and you head over the sea on this most difficult expedition. As you reach your destination you may be assured that your honor and greatness will be remembered. You have proved to be the greatest inspiration and we offer our appreciation as you go.

After a month's operations the enemy carriers were seen yesterday and they should be returning to port. The key to success in your enterprise is secrecy as you struggle to reach your destination in spite of the enormous difficulty of the weather.

As to each unit commander, although success must be certain, if for some reason true plans go askew we shall do our best to arrange for another attempt.

Finally, remember that there is no need for haste.

Let the soul of the gods be with you this day. We do not have to witness your unselfish loyalty and devotion. The many years of your training have provided a skill that makes it certain you will succeed with the aid of the divine spirit as you go to your eternal rest.[6]

The message read, the ceremony was nearly over. Admiral Ugaki posed for pictures with the young men. They now began to have reports from the four planes that had set off earlier to check the weather and patrol locally to be sure the unit was not surprised near home. The Kawanishi flying boats were already on their way. The enthusiasm of the Azuza Unit was very high. In an atmosphere of exaltation they boarded their aircraft, surrounded by the waving and cheering men of the air base. By 8:30 A.M. the Azuza Special Attack Unit planes were all off the ground and heading south, destination Ulithi. All was well.

But an hour later Admiral Ugaki received another message from Admiral Toyoda. The carriers had left Ulithi. Nobody knew where they had gone. Only a handful of ships and one carrier were in the harbor. That was not enough to justify the cost.[7]

Admiral Ugaki did not then know it, but Tokyo naval headquarters was in a state of total confusion. On the night before, as he had been banqueting the young heroes of the Azuza Unit, American B-29s had staged a new sort of air raid on Tokyo, three hundred aircraft carrying incendiaries and bombing from very low altitude. The raid had come in the middle of a storm, and high winds had accelerated the fury of the fire bombs and created a fire storm that swept through whole districts of Tokyo, destroying houses, burning buildings, and killing perhaps two hundred thousand people in a night of total terror. A quarter of a million houses were destroyed in this one night.[8]

So on the following morning the admirals were bemused by the new development in the war, and they were obviously not thinking very clearly. They panicked at the report from Truk without double checking and decided that the mission should be delayed, although it was already in mid-passage.

The entire mission was scrubbed in midair. The Kawanishi flying boats were called back in, and so were the twenty-four young pilots who had already steeled themselves to expect death at the end of the flight. To add to the frustration and pain was the word received shortly after the planes had all landed that there had been fifteen carriers in Ulithi on March 10, plus many other ships.

The fliers of the Azuza Unit were emotionally exhausted. They had geared themselves up for a supreme sacrifice, and now it all had to be done over again. There was no way that Admiral Ugaki could repeat the performance of the night before, the splendid banquet and the speeches and the fine sentiments of self-sacrifice. He did not even try.[9]

The Azuza Unit set out again the following morning, without ceremony this time. Again there was confusion and delay. The exhaustion and the tension showed on the faces of the young men as Admiral Ugaki again gave the ceremonial sake and the toast and bid them good luck on their mission. But finally they got off, with the flying boats out in front.

The futility of the mission was underscored by its performance. The weather grew worse, and one by one planes began to drop out of the formation. Engine trouble was one reason. Lack of enthusiasm was certainly another, but one that was never discussed. Eleven planes dropped out and landed on Japanese-held islands on the route south. Two more were ditched at sea. By the time the Azuza Unit reached the Ulithi area, there were only eleven attackers.[10]

They approached the atoll in the late afternoon, the clouds so thick they could not see the water or the islands below. After much circling and searching, they finally located land as dusk was falling. It turned out to be Yap, and they reoriented themselves and flew the short distance to Ulithi. The flying boats were now running low on fuel, and if they wanted to get back to Japan, as they were ordered to do, they must leave now. So they did. Thus, one element of the mission was already scrapped, the mission of reporting on results.

The pilots of the attack force flew on and approached Ulithi after darkness had fallen. They found the anchorage lighted. The Americans had so much confidence that they did not even black out this rear base. There below them were the carriers. The Japanese also had the advantage of total surprise. But it did not help.

The first plane peeled off over the brightly lighted harbor and made its attack on the carrier *Randolph*. The carrier was unguarded; only a handful of men were on watch. The rest were at the evening movies. The plane screamed down and its bomb exploded but did very little damage, and the plane did not explode because it had almost run out of gas.

That was the real story of the Azuza mission: Out of gas. The planes had flown one-third farther than they had expected, and most of them did not have enough gas to make an attack. They splashed ignominiously into the sea and were gone. None of them did any more damage. The mission was a total failure. Most puzzling to the Japanese high command was the lack of information from the enemy. Usually the Americans were punctilious about reporting on attacks and the progress of battles. But from Ulithi this night came nothing at all.[11]

On March 12 a scout plane from Truk got a good look at the Ulithi base in the morning sun and discovered nothing at all. The harbor was still full of ships, and not one of them appeared to be sunk or even damaged. And that is how it remained. The attack for which Admiral Toyoda and Imperial General Headquarters had nurtured such high hopes had come to nothing. The Americans did not even know they had been attacked by a special attack corps unit. Nothing at all, it was as if it had all been a dream.

Admiral Ugaki was first in despair; then, as he considered the tasks before him, he was filled with a renewed determination to give his every effort to the lost. Each time he sent a group of bright young pilots on their way to certain death, he felt a pang. He assuaged these pangs by making frequent trips to the temple to pray for the souls of the young men he was committing to death and to reiterate his resolute commitment to follow them to heaven and the spirits of his ancestors. To Ugaki, life had become no more than a prelude to death. His entire world had disappeared with the Imperial Navy, and what was left now was the effort to seek the survival of Japan and the Japanese people by the remnants of the armed forces that had served them so badly. Every day the consciousness of his failures rode heavily on the admiral's shoulders. He had failed his Emperor and he had failed the people of Japan. Everything he did now was an attempt to expiate those sins and to strike one blow that would somehow help to relieve the burden.

Falling Like Cherry Blossoms into the Sea

It was now almost mid-March, and the Japanese army and navy still had no unified command or unified plan for defense of the homeland. Since January the generals and the admirals had been meeting more or less continuously to create a combined defense. The army seemed to have a better idea than the navy about the strength of the American enemy. The generals estimated the American carrier strength at between seventeen and nineteen carriers, plus about fifty small carriers. To face this force the Japanese still had six ships that could be called carriers, but most of them were either converted seaplane tenders or not completed. And the army knew that in spite of much talk from the navy, there was no hope that the Combined Fleet could be reconstituted or a carrier force put into action.

In addition to the planes that were already available (and the army had about three times as many as the navy), the Japanese factories were turning out aircraft at the rate of two thousand per month, a very high figure made possible only because almost all defense production was now concentrated on aircraft.

Since January the army had been operating under a new defense plan. The army had drawn a great circle covering Japan, Manchuria, and North China. This area, said the army, could be defended because it was basically continuous. They disregarded the problem of getting from the Japanese islands to the Asian mainland; they contended that their command of the Sea of Japan, which had been a Japanese lake for forty years, would remain. (That spring American submarines began to prove them wrong.) They had already written off both Taiwan and Okinawa, although both islands were to be defended to the death by the current garrisons—and in the case of Taiwan this meant more than a million men, many of whom had been brought down from the Kwantung Army. Their plan was called Operation Ketsu—Decisive Operation.[1]

The navy came to the meetings with its own plan, which had spawned Admiral Ugaki's new operation. It called for massive attacks on the enemy's next invasion operation, whether it be at Okinawa, Taiwan, on the China coast, or in Kyushu. Obviously the Japanese were thinking along the same lines as the Allies; they were examining all the options and preparing for any of them. The navy's plan was called Operation Ten Go—Operation Heaven. Neither side would budge, so the idea of cooperation between the services remained only on the surface, given lip service but little else. The army stubbornly insisted on holding its major air forces for attack in the Ketsu Perimeter. The navy stubbornly insisted that the way to win the peace—no one talked now of winning the war—was to fight the enemy wherever he next came.

So in January the army prepared a new China offensive that was supposed to link Manchuria with Malaya, enabling the army to deliver supplies from one end to the other. It was not so wild a dream. In the next few months the army did run a corridor down the China coast, wiping out most of the Chinese and American air bases in East China. But on the surface the army and navy agreed and took a combined operations plan to the Emperor, which he approved. It called for defense of Okinawa, Iwo Jima, Taiwan, and the Great Circle of the army. It also noted that the two services expected the final battle to be fought in the Japanese home islands, and to that end the air strength would be conserved. But, in fact, the

army had no intention of sending any more strength to Okinawa or Taiwan, and the navy had no intention of conserv-
ing its air strength for the final battle. What the Emperor
approved was a plan of dreams, not reality. The only area in
which there was any real unity was in the decision that the
suicide game must be played from now on. In fact, the army
had been using suicide tactics ever since the Marianas:
Volunteers had been strapping explosives to their bodies and
diving under tanks. Since the days of the China war the
ultimate effort on behalf of the Emperor had always been
exalted by the services, and many a pilot had dived his plane
into a ship or an enemy position when the plane was stricken.
This kind of heroism was common to all nations, but from
the beginning the Japanese had taken it one step further and
lionized those who gave their lives when to others it might
not seem strictly necessary. The army had adopted that
principle, moved to the kamikaze suicide flight principle, and
now was going farther. The navy kamikazes had all been volunteers to this point, but in the winter of 1945 the army
began assigning men to suicide units. Any who indicated that
they were reluctant to die for the Emperor were put in the
forefront, to be gotten rid of on the first possible suicide
missions.[2]

The navy as yet had no such problem. There were plenty
of young pilots who were eager to give their all for the
Emperor. Admiral Ugaki's basic task was to find the best way
to employ them. After the ignominious failure of the Tan
Mission, Admiral Ugaki made a study of the reasons behind
the failure. He listed three reasons for the failure:

In the first place, the abortive mission of March 10 had started
things off all wrong. The entire operation had taken too much time,
and the suicide pilots were under too much tension because of it.

The second problem was caused by a change in the conditions of
the American ship anchorage in Ulithi, which caused some confusion when the pilots finally arrived on the scene.

Third, the organization of the mission left much to be desired.

The flying boats and weather scouts' reports had not proved very useful. The flying boats were delayed again on the morning of the mission, and they encountered tail winds and then had trouble finding the main body of the force. That caused another delay. Departure time difficulties and other problems threw the entire attack schedule off.

And then when the planes got into the air, their concern for avoiding enemy patrol planes and fighters was so great that it became a negative factor in the attack. More than it ought to have been.

The result was vacillation, indecision, and final failure.

Admiral Ugaki hoped by this report to avoid future interference in operations from the naval authorities in Tokyo. He wanted them to understand that it was their function to make policy but that operations were a delicate matter, and operations of suicide missions were extremely so.[3]

After the Tan Mission, Admiral Ugaki turned his attention to preparations for the future of the Fifth Air Fleet. He was given the responsibility for response to attacks on the southern islands, which meant the Ryukyus and Okinawa. It was here that he expected the next blow to come, and there was very little time to prepare. He had eight air groups in various stages of training; from them he must develop a fighting force. He had very little time. On March 13 Admiral Ugaki was tracking the movements of ships coming out of the Ulithi anchorage. He was thinking about making another try at Ulithi, but Imperial Headquarters would not approve. He must conserve his air strength for a great smash against the Allies when they made a new landing.

On March 15 Admiral Ugaki knew that a large American force was at sea. However, Japanese aerial scouting had been so reduced in recent months by the loss of bases that he was unable to find the aircraft carriers, so he went about his routine business, inspecting various units under his command and waiting for word of the whereabouts of the American carrier fleet. It was the same on March 16, and on March 17 he took time out to go pheasant hunting. When he returned to the hotel in Kagoshima from the expedition a message was waiting from Tokyo, brought by a staff officer who had flown with it from the Kanoya base. The enemy carrier force was moving north, Admiral Toyoda said, having left Ulithi on March 14.

Ugaki called off his scheduled activities for the day and flew back to Kanoya after lunch to make plans for operations. That night search planes found three task groups, including carriers, southeast of Kyushu. These were three of Admiral Marc Mitscher's Task Force 58, which was coming to make an attack on the Kyushu airfields preliminary to the invasion of Okinawa.

That night, as Admiral Mitscher's carriers moved to the point from which they would launch air strikes on the morning of March 18, Admiral Ugaki moved into the underground operations room at Kanoya to prepare for battle. Soon he was on the telephone to Hiyoshi, where the Combined Fleet headquarters was located just outside Tokyo. Admiral Toyoda and the other naval chiefs were trying to figure out how to cope with the American task force. They had come to no conclusion. This was not very helpful to Admiral Ugaki, who had to deal with the matter. Before midnight Ugaki's search planes had established the fact that the enemy consisted of four task groups.[4]

Ugaki had a confusing assortment of messages from Hiyoshi. One suggested an invasion of Okinawa, to which the Combined Fleet would respond, it said, with all its strength. This would be Operation Ten No. 1. But this heroic message was immediately followed by another, which was much less specific. If the enemy task force attacked the Kanto Plain area, then nothing would be done, to preserve the air strength for the future. It might mean a direct attack next on Japan proper. If the enemy attacked Kyushu, the scenario would be the same: Preserve the aircraft in case a landing on Kyushu came next.

But if the enemy attacked in the Okinawa area, the response was to be quite different. "However, when it becomes certain that the enemy will invade the southwest islands, positive operations will be adopted to destroy the enemy attempt by all means." But at the end of that message was another provision that applied specifically to Admiral Ugaki's command. "However, those strengths of the First Land-Based Air Task Force—that is, the Fifth Air Fleet deployed in the Kyushu area—will continue operations against enemy task forces as before, based upon the said operational policy, until the new deployment is completed."

What that gobbledygook meant was that Admiral Ugaki was to build his air strength for the ultimate invasion of Kyushu, but he was also to take the sole responsibility for destruction of the enemy task forces wherever they might strike. He was told, in other words, to conserve his aircraft but to expend them. Obviously it was impossible to do both jobs simultaneously, and Admiral Ugaki, being a fighting man, chose to honor the second part of the order, which was to carry the battle to the enemy.[5]

Just before 4 o'clock on the morning of March 18, Admiral Ugaki received the confusing message and had to make a decision about what to do. From the previous experience of February on the Kanto Plain he could expect such relentless attacks on the Japanese airfields of Kyushu that planes would not be able to operate from the fields. He hated to see the planes destroyed on the ground, so he decided to make a maximum air effort against the task force.

The night attack force of twin-engined bombers took off just before 4 o'clock in the morning. They got away from the fields just in time, because half an hour later the American carrier planes began to arrive. They were puzzled not to find any aircraft about. They began to work over the buildings and airfield installations.

The planes of the night attack force found Rear Admiral Arthur Radford's force three hours later and began to attack.

The American carriers were operating about 75 miles south of Shikoku. The planes came in and one bombed the *Enterprise*, but the bomb did not explode. A twin-engined bomber tried to crash on the *Intrepid*. It was shot down, but it fell so close to the ship that two men were killed and forty-three wounded by the explosion. Part of the bomber fell into the hazard deck, where it did some damage. Three bombers of the morning attack force, which left Kyushu at 6 o'clock in the morning, also found the carrier force and attacked the *Yorktown*. One dropped a bomb that went through the signal bridge to the deck below and exploded, blowing two big holes in the ship and killing five men and wounding another twenty-six.

Once again, all day long the American carrier planes ranged over Kyushu and Shikoku islands, doing a great deal of damage to airfield installations but not hitting many planes, which were secreted or in the air trying to attack the American forces. In this attack Admiral Ugaki lost fifty planes. He wanted to launch a dusk attack but there were too many American planes over the airfields, so a night attack was chosen instead. However, because of the confusion engendered by the all-day attacks of the Americans, he could not get the special unit that had been assembled, the Shinrai Special Attack Group, to be ready to take off. So the mission was scrubbed.

All night long the Japanese search planes were out, and early in the morning of March 19 the attack planes again found an American carrier group, Task Group 58.2 this time. In the first attack they hit the carrier *Wasp*, which had just sent two-thirds of her planes off on strikes into the Inland Sea, where they would find and damage the *Yamato*, Admiral Ugaki's old flagship. The Japanese planes managed to come in under the combat air patrol screen. Unseen by the anti-aircraft gunners, they dropped a bomb that hit the hangar deck and caused a plane to explode there, passed through the crew quarters on the deck below, and exploded on the mess deck, killing many cooks and mess attendants.

Casualties were heavy—more than a hundred men killed and almost three hundred wounded. The water mains failed when fires broke out on five decks simultaneously. But by 8 o'clock that morning the *Wasp* had begun to recover planes. Another bomb nearly hit the carrier and caused some more casualties. But the *Wasp* continued to operate for several days before she went back to Ulithi for repairs.[6]

Next the kamikazes and regular attack planes went after the carrier *Franklin*, which was Admiral R. E. Davison's flagship. She was hit by two bombs from a plane that got under the screen. They created huge fires on the hangar deck, wrecked both elevators on the flight deck, and spread through the planes that were getting ready to take off. Soon the entire ship was aflame and covered by heavy smoke. The planes, ammunition, and bombs began to explode. Admiral Mitscher's flagship was many miles away, out of sight, but she could hear the explosions aboard the *Franklin*. Admiral Davison shifted his command to the *Hancock*. The captain told most of the men to abandon ship but made an effort to save it, and the effort succeeded after many hours of fire fighting. However, the *Franklin* was out of action for the rest of the war. Her casualties were almost 750 men. So Ugaki's force had achieved a considerable success in doing major damage to two carriers.

Admiral Ugaki had planned for more attacks later in the day, but the weather grew very bad and they had to be suspended. The search planes kept fairly good track of the American carrier forces, however, and found them again that evening south of Cape Muroto. The 701st Air Group was sent out to attack in the afternoon and again found Admiral Davison's task force. They attacked, and one burning Zero aimed for the flight deck of the carrier *Hancock*. It missed and crashed into the destroyer *Halsey Powell*, killing twelve men and wounding twenty-nine. The plane's bomb went through the ship and did not explode. That evening in more attacks fires were started on the deck of the *Enterprise*.[7]

The pilots of the 701st were skilled units and were not constrained to make suicide attacks. As Admiral Ugaki wrote in his diary,

some skilled *suisei* pilots, regretting the result of their attacks could not be confirmed, made a low-altitude bombing and confirmed their attacks amidship on an enemy vessel. After returning to base, they immediately reloaded bombs and started out on another attack. With skilled pilots this method is more economical and effective. However, if we applied this in general [such was the skill level of most pilots], we wouldn't be able to expect a sure hit. This is a very difficult point with which to cope. I believe, however, that we still must place more importance on the spirit of the special attack [i.e., suicide attack].

But for the moment he relaxed the strictures for these skillful pilots. "Seeing the noticeable result being achieved, I encouraged them to repeat more fierce attacks, but only a small number of navy bombers, Gingas and Tenzans, were available, so achieved few results."

Already Ugaki was beginning to come under the pressures engendered by the suicide system, which put all concerned into a state of continual tension. When the commander of one group of suicide forces learned about Ugaki's praise for the conventional bombers, he announced that he would have to commit ritual suicide because the words reflected so badly on his suicide air group and their efforts. That statement could be discounted; very few officers who threatened to commit *seppuku* actually did so, but it emphasized the difficulties Admiral Ugaki now faced in managing this complicated air command. In this case Ugaki invited the commander to commit suicide, and no more was heard of the matter.

By this time the Oka flying bomb had been perfected, that small aircraft with a built-in explosive charge that was carried by a mother plane to the point of attack and then loosed. It was a 5,000-pound weapon with a small rocket engine that would carry it to the target, and no landing gear. It was a suicide weapon pure and simple. The first time Admiral

Ugaki had seen one of these "baka bombs"—fool bombs—he had been in awe and a little chagrined that the war had come to such a pass, but now he accepted them as part of his arsenal. He made plans to employ the Oka against the retreating American task forces that night of March 20.[8]

On the morning of March 21 search and attack planes reported torpedoing a cruiser east of Kyushu, but it must have been an illusion. That day Admiral Ugaki made the first use of his Shinrai unit, a group of twin-engined bombers that carried Oka flying bombs and had trained in putting them into use. This force consisted of eighteen twin-engined bombers, sixteen of them carrying Okas. They took off at 11:30 A.M., escorted by some thirty fighters. Admiral Ugaki waited impatiently for news of their success, but late in the afternoon the fighters returned with a sad story. Virtually all of the twin-engined bombers were shot down before they could launch their Okas. The flying bombs made them so heavy that they were easy prey for the American fighters.

Thus, another weapon in which Imperial General Headquarters had invested much time and energy was proved to be faulty. Eighteen bombers and their crews, plus eight suicide pilots, went to their deaths without producing any results.

Even so, early in the game Admiral Ugaki had hardened himself to these needless deaths. His promise to himself, which he repeated several times in his diary, was that at some point he would follow the young men he was sending to certain death and be united with their spirits in heaven.

The American task force moved away from the Japanese islands, bound for Okinawa where it would support the coming invasion. Admiral Ugaki summed up the results, or what the Japanese thought were the results:

5 carriers

2 battleships

1 heavy cruiser

2 cruisers

1 unidentified ship—

ALL SUNK![9]

Admiral Ugaki had been listening on the radio as the pilots bored in to make their attacks, and he had heard many of them say, "I am going to ram a carrier," or "I am just ramming a carrier," so he believed that eight carriers had been sunk or badly damaged. But when the report reached Combined Fleet headquarters, the staff cut the claim to four ships sunk. When that report reached Imperial General Headquarters, the claim was cut to two.

The losses of the Japanese air forces in this first military operation of the new command had been very high: 161 planes lost of 193 aircraft committed to action. The Americans also claimed to have destroyed more than 500 planes on the ground and in the air.[10]

As the Americans geared up for the invasion of Okinawa, the Japanese air defenses were getting organized. The Combined Fleet issued a citation to the Fifth Air Fleet for its excellent work during the American air raids on the main islands. Although Admiral Ugaki felt that it was more than was deserved by the results, he was pleased for the effect the citation had on morale.

The movement of the American fleet put an end to four straight days of battle. Admiral Ugaki returned to his shack on the hillside above the Kanoya field. "Spring was everywhere, and fatigue from the battle disappeared immediately. Nature's great progress in a few days' time seemed to laugh pityingly at the silly little human world, where we are making a fuss about war."

As March neared its end the Americans moved toward Okinawa with a huge invasion force, while Admiral Ugaki made preparations for the coming battle.

Operation Ten Go

On Sunday, March 25, 1945, the American air raids and bombardment of Okinawa were so fierce that the Japanese knew the invasion was coming momentarily. Minesweeping operations could be seen from Naha, and a landing was made on Kerama Island about 15 miles away. The Americans wanted the Kerama Retto, a small group of islands, for a fuel and ammunition depot for the Okinawa invasion. Admiral Toyoda then alerted the naval forces for Operation Ten Go, part one. This order placed Admiral Teraoka's Third Air Fleet under the general command of Admiral Ugaki as head of the air defense of the homeland.[1]

When Admiral Ugaki received that order, he issued orders for a major kamikaze effort to be made on the night of March 26. He had no immediate plans to employ Admiral Teraoka's forces because they were not well enough trained, so that element remained largely as a training command. On March 25 one unit attacked the American fleet units and claimed two battleships, but actually only one destroyer was hit and the torpedo that struck it passed through the ship and exploded on the other side, doing very little damage. On March 26 nine kamikazes tried to crash ships in the Kerama Retto area, but they all failed to make contact and were wasted. Early on the morning of March 27 one kamikaze damaged the destroyer *Kimberley*. Later in the day one kamikaze crashed on the battleship *Nevada* and another on the light cruiser *Biloxi*, and they damaged the destroyer *O'Brien* and the destroyer minelayer *Dorsey*. Admiral Ugaki knew they had sacrificed seventeen aircraft. The army had also sent some planes to Kerama Retto.

In conjunction with the Okinawa landings, Admiral Nimitz demanded support from the B-29 bombers, and on March 27 they hit the Kyushu airfields, destroying a large number of training planes at Tachiari air base.

Almost every day the kamikazes attacked some Allied ships, but their efforts were largely in vain. Only minimal damage was recorded by the Americans. In turn, the carriers of Admiral Mitscher's task group visited Kyushu and hit airfields in March 28 and March 29, doing some damage.[2]

Admiral Ugaki's headquarters became the hub of the air defense, and a constant stream of callers arrived from the army and from other naval units.

On March 31 Admiral Ugaki stepped up the tempo of the kamikaze operations. The basic problem for his command, however, was the securing of factual information about the success or failure of the attacks. Many claims were made, but some of the real successes were not known to the Japanese. One was the successful attack on March 31 on the cruiser *Indianapolis*, which was the flagship of Admiral Raymond Spruance, commander of the Okinawa invasion. Spruance and his staff were unhurt, but they had to transfer their operations to the battleship *New Mexico* and the *Indianapolis* had to return to the United States for repair.

Every day in early April some kamikazes set out. They hit ships, mostly transports and destroyers and the smaller vessels, although the carriers were their announced game. They did damage continually, but not enough to affect the outcome of the battle raging ashore on Okinawa. Each day Ugaki sent out thirty to fifty aircraft, and each day the returning pilots came back with claims, usually overinflated.

But on April 3 a destroyer was hit, an LST was knocked out, and the escort carrier *Wake Island* had a hole blown in her side and had to retire to Guam for repairs.

In the first week of April Admiral Ugaki was preparing for his big attack, Kikusui No. 1. The attack came on April 6. A first wave of 27 fighter planes flew high to lure Allied fighters up high while the second, third, and fourth waves, each of 27 planes, patrolled above the island and 40 army fighters flew air patrol to the island. A total of 110 naval special attack planes (kamikazes) attacked the fleet then, plus 90 army kamikazes and more planes of the Eighth Air Division and the First Air Fleet. Their success included 3 destroyers, 2 ammunition ships, and an LST sunk; 9 destroyers and a minelayer badly damaged; and many other ships damaged. On the same day the battleship *Yamato*, on which Ugaki had served first as Combined Fleet chief of staff and then as battleship division commander, set out for Okinawa with the mission of beaching there and turning herself into a fortress from which the enemy would be resisted to the last. But the *Yamato* never made it to Okinawa. She was found by American carrier planes and sunk ignominiously without a chance to use her big guns.

Admiral Ugaki greeted the news sadly:

The Surface Special Attack Force thus met a tragic end before reaching its destination. While *Yamato* was Fleet Admiral Yamamoto's flagship I was on board her for one full year as his chief of staff. Later she served as my flagship of the First Battleship Division from May 1944 and participated in the Biak campaign, the battle of the Philippine Sea, and also in the battle of Leyte Gulf, before I was ordered home in late November last year. My dear *Yamato* finally went down in the China Sea.[3]

Operation Ten Go No. 1 continued. Navy and army planes by the score went against the American fleet on April 7, hitting the battleship *Maryland*, the carrier *Hancock*, two destroyers, and some lesser vessels. The damage was serious, but it did not stop the American fleet.

The seriousness of the war situation was underlined by the collapse of the Koiso cabinet. This government had served for eight months following the sacking by the Emperor of General Hideki Tojo, but it had been unable to make any progress in ending the war. So a cabinet dominated by the navy was to be tried. Kantaro Suzuki, president of the Privy Council, was a retired admiral, and he was chosen to form a new cabinet that was heavily loaded with admirals.

"Now that the good-natured navy is going to take charge of the state at this time of agony, I hope they will govern forcefully," wrote Admiral Ugaki in his diary, "because it was the unanimous voice of the people at present. The navy, now without ships, is going to fight at the critical time by forming a cabinet with its predecessors. Ah! Ha!"[4]

As the kamikaze waves continued, the reporting to Ugaki became totally inaccurate. But by April 10 his claim was that 169 capital ships had been sunk or badly damaged, plus many transports. So he regarded the Kikusui No. 1 operation as a great success. On the basis of such erroneous reports Admiral Toyoda predicted that Japan had a fifty-fifty chance of winning the battle for Okinawa.

Kikusui No. 2 was supposed to follow directly on No. 1, but bad weather slowed the Japanese suicide forces down. Attacks began again on April 11, and the results were very good according to the reports. Actually, the battleship *Missouri*, the carrier *Enterprise*, and several smaller ships were hit. Ugaki's problem was that there were too many ships. At Guadalcanal he had written, "We continue to destroy the enemy, but he keeps sending more ships." And this was true now, too. "Every day we try to finish the enemy task force, and yet they can't be finished."

Kikusui No. 2 began on April 12. It was another assault by wave after wave of kamikazes. By this time Admiral Ugaki had the entirely erroneous idea that he had half crippled the American naval force. "At about 1330 three groups of enemy carriers, consisting of six regular ones and two converted ones, were at a point 60 to 80 miles east of the northern tip of Okinawa. They seem to be still powerful, but they'll be all their remaining forces. I want to wipe them out by any means."[5]

This day the army and navy did cooperate. Fifteen fighters from the army went in the first wave. Then came three waves each of twenty-four navy fighters. Thirty-four fighters of Commander Minoru Genda's 343rd Air Group also went out. They were skilled pilots, among the few left in Japan. Even so, twelve of the thirty-four did not come back.

Ugaki also sent an attack force of Okas this day, as well as sixty army kamikazes and many other planes. At the end of the day Admiral Ugaki reported that they had sunk two cruisers, set a battleship on fire, and torpedoed another battleship. Altogether nearly four hundred planes had attacked the Americans, about half of them kamikazes, and nearly half had been shot down by the carriers and their planes. They had sunk several ships and damaged a larger number, including the battleship *Tennessee*. But they had not hit a carrier.[6]

The Okas were proving to be a big disappointment, although high hopes had been held for them. Time and again they were used, but the only success was on April 12 when an Oka sank the destroyer *Mannert L. Abele*. All the others were wasted, and usually their parent bombers were shot down too.

Admiral Ugaki persisted in his optimism about the results of his suicide plane campaign. He believed that President Roosevelt, who died on April 13, had died as a result of the success of Operation Ten Go. With good heart, the string of suicidal attacks continued.[7]

Admiral Morishita, with whom Admiral Ugaki had served in the battleship days, came to call. They commiserated on the loss of the *Yamato* and the foolishness of the Naval

General Staff, which had planned the suicidal foray of the battleship. They also commiserated on the disbanding of the Second Fleet, which had made the attack on Leyte Gulf, but Ugaki professed optimism about the results of the suicide corps.

How much of this was bravado cannot be known, but certainly a good deal of it must have been. Ugaki was too old a hand at interpreting the inflated claims of fliers to believe all the reports that came in about sinkings of battleships and carriers. If the reports were all true, the entire American fleet would already be at the bottom of the sea. There was nothing to be done but to make as much sense of the reports as possible and to send observation planes with the suicide forces whenever possible, hoping they would get back to put the record straight on results. Another factor that weighed the sifting of the evidence was the reluctance of the high officers to see young men going to death uselessly, so they tended to weight the evidence for the claimants.

The war was going very badly. Everybody knew that. The fact was emphasized for Admiral Ugaki by news from his family in Tokyo. They wanted to evacuate and move out of the capital area to escape the B-29 bombing. But he asked them not to desert the house. His reason was patriotic, not personal. He cared nothing for the house, for he intended to die before the war ended. But he felt that for a man of some position to desert the capital showed a certain disloyalty that would have an effect on people. However, in the end he had to think of his family and he instructed them on how to dispose of his Tokyo house.

By April 15 two Kikusui operations of mass suicide attack had been completed, and Ugaki and the high command professed themselves satisfied enough with the program to launch the third wave.

Kikusui No. 3 began at noon on April 16, again starting with search planes and then fighters to try to keep the enemy fighters away while the suicide planes attacked. The results again were overemphasized by the Japanese, but the fact was that the carrier *Intrepid* was hit and put out of action and other ships were hit. The toll of the kamikazes was rising; it was a subject of more than a little concern in Washington, at Pearl Harbor, and at the advance base in Guam. The U.S. Navy searched for quick remedies but never did find any. There could be no response to a system in which men were willing to steer their aircraft into a ship and kill themselves to do it, except to maintain constant vigilance and make every attempt to stop the suicide planes before they could come within range to attack. All these actions were taken, yet some planes continued to get through. The very number of them precluded stopping them all.

By April 17, relying on the reports of his intelligence officers, Admiral Ugaki concluded that one more big push with the wave attacks would finish the American carrier force. But his key officers were exhausted, and the units that he would have to send to death were not yet ready for the plunge. So reluctantly he called off further strikes for the moment.[8]

The talk was all about Okinawa, but the thinking was all about the future and what would be very definitely the Decisive Battle, the battle for Japan to be fought on the beaches and in the skies of Japan itself. Even as they fought the battle of Okinawa, all those entrusted with the defense of Japan were thinking about Operation Ketsu—Decisive Operation. The B-29s were working over the airfields of Japan these days, which meant to the Japanese that the Americans were also planning for Operation Ketsu. There was no doubt about it. The B-29 attacks seriously disrupted Admiral Ugaki's air operations against Okinawa, as on April 18 when the superfortress raids did considerable damage to his home field at Kanoya and several other Kyushu air bases. Twenty of his airplanes were burned up and fifty were damaged.

By April 23 the B-29 raids and a number of raids by carrier-

based planes had brought the naval and army air forces to
new lows. In view of the concentration on Operation Ketsu,
the Combined Fleet decided that Ugaki's operations would
have to be cut back to conserve aircraft, and he was so
informed. *Shikata ganai!*—It can't be helped! There was
nothing to be done about it. There simply were not enough
aircraft being produced to make up for losses and build for
the decisive battle of the future. He had 620 aircraft available,
of which 370 were operational. That month the aircraft
plants produced 600 planes for the navy and 400 for the
army, a welcome ratio change that reflected the battle for
Okinawa. But many of those planes had to be saved for the
future, and so did gasoline supplies.

The Combined Fleet wanted another Tan Mission, an
attack on the Ulithi anchorage, to slow down the Americans'
advance. Ugaki was unwilling to do it from Kyushu, remem-
bering the last time, so he persuaded the Combined Fleet to
mount the operation from Truk, which was much more
sensible.

By May 1 Ugaki was committed to Kikusui No. 5, the
fifth wave of suicide planes to attack at Okinawa. The
Emperor had shown some interest in the announced successes
of the operations; this had prompted the woebegone General
Staff to continue them, although some members knew the
truth—that they were only destructive, and self-defeating in
a way. On May 1 Admiral Toyoda was appointed commander
in chief of the navy, taking on a number of new positions that
had never been held by one man before. It was an indication
of the growing feeling in Japan that only a unified action
would bring any chance of success.

By that time Kanoya was feeling the impact of constant
bombing, not only from B-29s and carrier-borne planes but
from B-25 medium army bombers that had been ranged up to
Okinawa and islands near Japan.[9]

Kikusui No. 5, which began on May 3 and continued into

May 4 and May 5, was as usual a success announced by the Japanese navy. As usual the effects were felt by the Allied fleet, because so many suicide planes had to have at least some successes. The Japanese claimed three battleships and at least four heavy cruisers. But they were wrong, as was almost always the case these days. However, they were hitting, damaging, and sinking the picket destroyers of the Allied force around Okinawa, and they were occasionally hitting a carrier. They struck the British carriers *Formidable* and *Indomitable*. But they learned that the British carriers were stronger than the American: They had steel flight decks that did not burn when hit.

From the beginning Kikusui No. 5 was adversely affected by the almost daily bombings of the airfields. Pitted runways, wrecked operations buildings, damaged planes, and uncertain takeoff times to escape the bombing were all problems that cut into the efficacy of the raids. On the night of May 4, seventy bombers attacked the vessels in port at Okinawa and the fleet units. In the morning the fighters came in four waves, and under their cover the suicide pilots attacked, sixty-four bombers and seven Okas.

Based on eyewitness accounts, Ugaki claimed three battleships and several heavy cruisers for this attack. Actually, the largest ship hit was the cruiser *Birmingham*; although she was only damaged, it was serious enough to send her away for repair. But the damage to destroyers and the sinking of destroyers, LCMs, LSTs, and other smaller vessels was considerable.[10]

May 7 was the date for the third Tan operation, the bombing of Ulithi, which once again was launched from Kanoya base by the Fourth Mitate Unit of the Kamikaze Special Attack Force. Once again it was a total failure. Of the twenty-one planes that took off, more than one-third failed even to reach the Ulithi area. By the time the flight commander neared the target there were only four planes following him, so he scrubbed the mission and returned to a Japanese base. Admiral Ugaki observed that the Japanese were reducing their own strength with their own hands and should stop trying to mount missions of 1,400 miles where they could not even forecast the weather conditions.

From the reports received from the army, Admiral Ugaki had the impression that the battle for Okinawa ashore was going rather well for the Japanese and that they had a chance to drive the Americans off the island. But generally speaking his pessimism about the war grew almost daily. Admiral Toyoda came down to Kanoya for a day or two and they discussed plans. Toyoda said he was going to appoint a large number of younger officers to high ranks and retire some of the old ones. All very well, said Ugaki, but how would that help win the war?

There was no real answer to that question. He and Toyoda agreed to put on the sixth Kikusui operation on May 11 and to try the No. 3 Tan operation once again, despite Ugaki's reservations about it.[11]

Kikusui No. 6 involved about fifty suicide planes, plus the usual flights of straight bombers, observation planes, and fighters to cover the suicide attacks. As a result two destroyers were disabled and the carrier *Bunker Hill* was hurt so badly she had to go to the United States for repairs. This was Admiral Mitscher's flagship, and in the attack 396 men were killed and 264 wounded.

But the American attacks on the Kyushu airfields were taking their toll. Men were becoming exhausted and careless. One fighter started to take off, swerved off the runway, and plowed through parked planes. Before the damage was finished eleven planes had burned. On May 11 the B-29 command, which had opposed flying missions against the airfields from the beginning, had its way and went back to firebombing Japanese cities after sending fifty B-29s against Kyushu. Some of the pressure was thus relieved, but by this time B-25 medium bombers could reach Kyushu from Okinawa and other Ryukyus bases. Admiral Ugaki was talking about the need to abandon the camps and dig underground so that the men could get a night's sleep, so ubiquitous was the bombing.

Ugaki often wondered why the high command thought they could win the war by shuffling the commands around. They did it again on March 12, combining his Fifth Air Fleet and the Third Air Fleet under his command as the Ten Air Force. This meant that he would have direct access to, and thus command of, the training force as well as the operational air forces. What difference it would make he did not know. It did not seem very hopeful.

The high command wanted more raids on Ulithi. As always, Ugaki was preoccupied with the whereabouts of the carriers, and just now he knew they were in his backyard and that he could expect more serious carrier raids in the next few days. To counter the forces he organized suicide air raids, which went out and, as usual, did some damage. On May 13 the destroyer *Bache* was hit by a suicide plane; forty-one men were killed and thirty-two wounded, and she had to be towed back to Kerama Retto. More attack planes went out on the night of May 13, but Ugaki had no report on their success. It was considerable: They hit the carrier *Enterprise*, Admiral Mitscher's new flagship, and damaged it so badly that it was out of the war for good. Mitscher transferred command to the carrier *Randolph*, and the carrier war went on.

By May 16 the American carriers had moved away from Japan and Ugaki could again turn his mind to offensive operations. But he lamented that nearly every day the fighting strength of his air force was decreasing because of the Americans' attacks. On May 15 four hundred B-29s bombed Nagoya, trying to destroy the Mitsubishi aircraft engine plant. They did not succeed. But they did a great deal of damage to the city and to other defense installations, besides burning down Nagoya castle. More important than the destruction of landmarks was the mining of the Inland Sea, which caused great shipping loss and affected Ugaki's air operations.

Doggedly Ugaki's air force kept after the Allied forces on and around Okinawa. Kikusui No. 7 was set for May 24 but was postponed at the eleventh hour because of bad weather. Later it was carried out when more carrier planes began to attack Kyushu again. This was an admitted failure. But Ugaki was already planning Kikusui No. 8.[12]

By May 25 Ugaki was noting that he was forced to use trainers, notoriously slow aircraft, in his attacks because he was running out of planes. This meant he had to rely even more heavily on fighter escort because the trainer planes, piloted by none too skillful young men, could not be expected to do much if they were also intercepted by enemy fighters.

By the end of May Ugaki's force was so straitened that much of the attack carried out in the Okinawa area was done by army planes, and their suicide attacks were even more wasteful and less productive than the navy's. Ugaki did not get direct information about the army results. On May 27 the army and the navy performed a joint operation, of which the navy's part was Kikusui No. 8. But what a difference there was now compared to the beginning, when first-line aircraft had been available. This day Ugaki sent off twenty-three trainers, fifteen seaplanes, six torpedo bombers, eleven twin-engined bombers, four dive bombers, and four other bombers. Another six bombers and eleven fighters would fly patrol and report missions. Several ships were damaged, the worst being a destroyer that was towed to Kerama Retto.

The last days of May 1945 were marked by a general deterioration of the weather as the spring rainy season came on. The B-29 attacks continued unabated. More and more small aircraft from Iwo Jima and the southern islands attacked Kyushu, carrying out what in effect became continual harassing raids. These were very troublesome to Ugaki's command and bothered his scheduling of operations. All Japan seemed to be on dead center. As Admiral Ugaki wrote in his diary on May 30, "When operations are prolonged and there's no strong spiritual stimulation, the general morale tends to be stagnant and dull. Especially, it was feared, the resumption of liberty after more than two months [which he had just reinstated] might cause them to misunderstand the battle situation."[13]

So the battle went on, but for the Japanese it was obviously a wearing and always losing battle. The air attacks on Okinawa continued even after the land fighting ended in June. Kikusui No. 9 was launched a few hours before the land fighting ended, but the weather forced the cancellation and the diversion of the planes to other projects. What was most remarkable was the paucity of planes employed. In the first Kikusui operations the waves had numbered in the hundreds. Now they were in the tens. And on June 3, the day of Kikusui No. 9, only one small ship, a landing craft tank, was damaged at Okinawa. Most infuriating to Ugaki was a growing sense of helplessness. It was underlined early in June when he was inspecting an installation overlooking Kagoshima Bay: He watched while an American PBM flying boat came over the bay, circled, and landed to pick up the crewmen of a bomber shot down over the bay that morning.

"I can't stand even to see an enemy submarine picking up survivors off shore, much less this arrogant behavior right in the middle of Kagoshima Bay," wrote Admiral Ugaki.[14]

This was the forty-third month of the Pacific war, and although Admiral Ugaki could not stand to see such things happening, there was absolutely nothing he could do to stop them.

The Long Summer

Admiral Ugaki was preparing for defeat and for death. He received new honor from the throne. He was promoted to the senior grade of fourth court rank, "an honor to be cherished" but not really meaningful to him at this point. He learned also that in 1944 when he was overseas he had been awarded the First Order of the Sacred Treasure. It was appreciated but not really germane to the day's affairs. He was drawn ever more closely to nature, as is the Japanese way when crisis threatens, and he filled his diary with comments about the wheat crop, rainfall, fireflies, and cuckoos. He sent the completed sections of his war diary and uniforms to Okayama, where he had been born. Every day he was preparing for the end.[1]

Early in June the pressure on Japan stepped up when Admiral William F. Halsey took over the fleet, which was called the Third Fleet under his command. He reversed the purely defensive role the fleet had taken under Admiral Raymond Spruance. Halsey believed that the best way to counteract the kamikazes that harried the American forces in what was now their most forward base of Okinawa was to conduct a spirited offense and destroy the Japanese air power at its sources. So he moved the fleet back into Japanese waters and stayed there.[2]

On June 9 Kikusui No. 9 was sent off. All that Ugaki could

muster for the attack was forty-six planes, and fewer than half were special attack planes. Only ten succeeded in making attacks. They claimed to have hit ten ships but damaged only one American destroyer. By this time, although the navy listed the air strength of Ugaki's command in the thousands of planes, he actually had about seven hundred in the Third and Fifth Air Fleets, and only about six hundred were operational. The picture was even gloomier than the statistics indicated. Most of his fliers were not skillful enough to make night operations. "It's very distressing," said Admiral Ugaki.[3]

He was equally distressed by the inactivity of many of the senior naval commanders, who were doing nothing but waiting for the decisive battle on the homeland front. As if in answer to his complaint the Grand Naval Command, the new operational command of the navy, ordered his Third Fleet to make an attack against the B-29s in the Marianas with forty twin-engined bombers.

Admiral Ugaki also continued operations at Okinawa, although he now knew with certainty that the battle was lost and that the naval command there had ceased to be in communication with either Tokyo or Kanoya.

Admiral Ugaki's problems were growing critical. On June 8 about eighty carrier planes from Task Force 38 attacked Kanoya while the Japanese were eating lunch. They destroyed many aircraft parked in shelters, burning several and putting holes in more than forty. But as serious as the problem of damage to aircraft was, more serious was the shortage of fuel caused by the mining of the Inland Sea and the air attacks on coastal shipping. Ugaki was unable to get a steady supply of fuel to Kanoya. On June 11, eleven B-24 bombers and thirty American fighters attacked Kanoya and were intercepted by forty Zeroes, but the Japanese did not shoot down a single American plane. The problem was lack of skill and lack of determination. What the pilots needed was training, but the fuel shortage was so great there was no fuel for training.[4]

Yet the attacks had to go on. On June 14 Ugaki launched Kikusui No. 10 in conjunction with a general attack by the army's Sixth Air Army. This time he would make extensive use of the Oka, he decided. But that day it rained very hard and the attack had to be canceled.

Meanwhile the American attacks continued unabated. The B-29s, having done as much damage as possible to the industrial areas of Osaka, Kobe, and Tokyo, now turned to smaller cities and sent waves of aircraft nearly every day, four hundred and more at a time. On June 18 Ugaki said they destroyed eighty thousand houses in Kagoshima. From reports he received after staff officers had made some trips around the country, Ugaki wondered if the Americans intended to destroy every city in Japan.[5]

Because of bombing, fuel problems, and above all because of weather, Kikusui No. 10 was delayed until June 22. Ugaki put together a mixed force of forty-seven suicide planes, twin-engine bombers, torpedo planes, obsolete fighters, observation planes, and training planes—all of which set off with only eight night fighters to protect them and report on their success. The results were slight; carriers were claimed but actually only two landing ships were hit and neither was sunk. Later in the day a small Oka force of six planes left and attacked the Naha district of Okinawa, but again the Okas were a disappointment.

Late in June Admiral Ugaki began to receive a string of army visitors. The reason was the preparation now beginning in earnest for Operation Ketsu, the final deciding battle on land, sea, and in the air over the shores of Japan itself. Some officers came to examine the defenses of the Kanoya area. Others came to discuss the air activity of Operation Ketsu. Half of Ugaki's time was now spent in such discussion and planning.

As far as defense was concerned, the lack of fuel and skilled pilots made it very difficult to offer any defense at all against the constant stream of attacking planes that came now from the Ryukyu land bases. Walking on the highway near his base, Ugaki saw ten American fighters circling his base and lazily peeling off to attack, with neither fighter interception nor anti-aircraft fire directed against them. The sight made him despair.

In July the American air attacks continued from carrier planes, B-29s, B-24s, B-25 medium bombers, and fighter planes all over Kyushu and in many parts of Honshu. Ugaki, who was constrained to conserve his forces for Operation Ketsu, did not even try to oppose them or strike back at the carriers off shore. His No. 2 Kanoya base was wrecked by attack early in July, but Ugaki did nothing but inspect the damage and report on it in his diary. In July the tempo of the American attacks on the Japanese homeland increased. The B-29s kept up their campaign of firebombing against secondary cities and even smaller places. The Halsey task force roamed up and down the Japanese shore, hitting the Tokyo area with a thousand planes and boasting about it, even naming some of the ships from which the attacks were launched, something they would never have done in the days when the Imperial Navy was a power to be reckoned with. The Halsey fleet also made surface bombardment attacks against the Japanese islands of Honshu and Hokkaido. There was absolutely no opposition, because everything for the army and the navy was being saved for Operation Ketsu. The American escort carrier *Anzio* and several surface escorts came up to the Japanese coast hunting submarines and sank the *I-13*, virtually in its own docking area. There was nothing to be done now about these attacks but to wait. But the frustration for such officers as Admiral Ugaki, who had been through the days of power, was so intense as to be almost unbearable.[6]

By mid-July Admiral Ugaki was moving farther afield, inspecting facilities that would play important roles in Operation Ketsu. He visited the 634th Air B Group and found it had concealed its operations in farm country; the aircraft were scattered and hidden. He visited Fifth Special Attack Squadron headquarters, which was a base for *kaiten* attack suicide submarines. He visited Tarumizu air base and the underground torpedo workshops that had been built there, and Shinjo, where special underground hangars had been constructed to build and house suicide surface boats.

Also in mid-July the carrier attacks ceased while the carriers went off to refuel and take on aircraft and ammunition, but they were back by July 24, concentrating on naval targets and trying to find aircraft, most of which were now artfully concealed. The Americans would never have believed it from what they saw, but the Japanese navy had more than five thousand planes available and the army admitted to more than four thousand and probably had twice as many. But not a plane rose to intercept the enemy as they ranged across the fields and towns of Japan. The only damage was the sinking of the destroyer *Underhill* that day by the submarine *I-53*. The air forces of army and navy were completely silent. The only air activity being carried out by Admiral Ugaki's force was the nightly dispatch of search planes to keep track of the enemy forces.[7]

At the end of July Admiral Ugaki began to move his headquarters from Kanoya to the Oita base, three and a half hours away by train, where he would be in a more centralized position to conduct the air operations of Operation Ketsu. He had been told that he would be appointed to a new command, the Combined Air Fleet, which would be the basic naval command for the defense of Japan. The other commands would be the suicide submarine and suicide surface boat commands. Everything was now devoted to that prospect. He expected to undergo another month of frustrating but not very successful Allied air attacks on Japanese installations before the Allies tried their landings.

On August 1 the navy had an unpleasant surprise. An enemy convoy was sighted off the coast of Japan, and some rattled staff officer in Tokyo panicked and announced the alert for Operation Ketsu. Everything in Japan was suspended for several hours until a search plane discovered that the "convoy" had only been phosphorescence seen on the sea. That same day the Americans launched their largest B-29 raids of the war using nearly nine hundred planes, but this was not nearly as much a matter of concern in Japan as the coming of an invasion fleet, which is what the false report indicated.[8] Nervousness permeated the Japanese military scene so deeply that such a simple phenomenon could produce so startling a result.

Admiral Ugaki and his staff arrived at Oita on August 2 and set up headquarters in an underground installation. He lived in a four-room house that belonged to a local farmer.[9]

The next few days were spent inspecting various installations and continuing to prepare for the final battle, which would begin the moment the Allies tried to invade the homeland.

The news continued to be more discouraging every day. On August 7 Admiral Ugaki learned about the dropping of the first atomic bomb on Hiroshima, and his immediate reaction was to try to conceive of some countermeasures to be taken against such bombs.

August 8 was devoted to table maneuvers, working out problems to be faced when the Allies tried their landings. The Allies continued air raids with B-29s and land-based aircraft from the Ryukyus against Kyushu.

On August 9 Admiral Ugaki was at Beppu Naval Hospital having a tooth treated when he learned that the Soviet Union was entering the war. This was a particular shock to Ugaki; since the days when he had served as a staff officer with the Naval High Command, he had worked and hoped for some sort of alliance with the Soviets, even when the army was bent on going to war with them. "Now this country is going to fight against the whole world," was Admiral Ugaki's reaction. "This is fate indeed!"[10]

On August 10 Ugaki received a report about the second

atomic bomb drop on Nagasaki from Captain Genda, who had seen it from Omura. On August 11 he learned with horror that San Francisco radio was talking about the possibility of a Japanese surrender. Ugaki shared the opinion of a number of high-ranking army officers that no matter what came now, the only solution for Japan was to conduct Operation Ketsu and make the enemy's assault on the Japanese homeland so expensive in terms of life and destruction that the enemy would lose heart.

"Even though it becomes impossible for us to continue organized resistance after expending our strength, we must continue guerrilla warfare under the Emperor and never give up the war. When this resolution is brought home, we can't be defeated. Instead we can make the enemy finally give up the war after making it taste the bitterness of a prolonged conflict."[11]

Personally, he renewed his resolution to die "as a samurai, an admiral, a supreme commander. I renew a resolution today of entrusting my body to the throne and defending the Empire until death takes me away."[12]

On August 12 Ugaki received a message from the Navy Ministry telling him to follow the national policy and warning that the government was embarked on peace negotiations. When he heard on the radio that the peace negotiations seemed to be failing he felt better, well enough to go to Beppu Hospital and have the just-finished crown on his tooth installed.

On August 13 Ugaki was again occupied with inspection of underground sites of fleet headquarters and other units. He received several orders concerning the conduct of Operation Ketsu, the reason being a concerted enemy air attack on the Kanto Plain by Halsey's carrier planes. Experience had taught the Japanese that these concerted attacks usually preceded a landing operation by not very many days.[13]

Because of all this activity in spite of orders to conserve aircraft, Ugaki sent some suicide planes to Okinawa on August 13. This was his last Okinawa operation, because Admiral Kusaka was succeeding him as commander of the fleet and Ugaki was moving up to command the entire air operation for the coming final battle. Ugaki felt that he should continue until this problem period was ended, but that matter was to be taken out of his hands.

He spent the night of August 13 in the bomb shelter at his headquarters waiting for news of the last attack. The next morning he was frustrated by the lack of information that prevented him from launching any attacks. And he knew the enemy carriers were still operating off Honshu. As Admiral Ugaki waited and waited and Kusaka never arrived, he heard foreign broadcasts about the military situation. By evening he knew that Japan seemed inclined to accept the Allied terms of surrender and that the use of atomic bombs had been suspended pending a Japanese reply to the Allied demands. He felt very gloomy, but that evening he gave a dinner party for the mayor of Oita, the town where his new headquarters was located, and they spoke of meeting again soon. Admiral Ugaki did not believe the words; he felt he would not be seeing many people again.

Late on the night of August 14 the Grand Naval Command flashed the alert for Operation Ketsu. The entire country was alerted for invasion then. The warning was that an enemy landing on the shores of Honshu could be very near at hand. But Admiral Ugaki disagreed. He did not think this was Ketsu, but an attempt by the fleet at sea to force the surrender of Japan. The daily air strike began at 4:45 on the morning of August 15, and American planes flew over Tokyo and attacked Tokurozama airfield on the Kanto Plain. They were called back by Halsey's announcement that Japan had surrendered, but the fighting did not end immediately. Several Japanese planes and several American planes were shot down in this last air battle of the war.[14]

The Grand Naval Command that day sent new orders to

Admiral Ugaki. There were to be no more attacks on the American fleet or on ships at Okinawa. The war was over.

Admiral Ugaki disagreed completely with these orders. He believed that Japan should fight to the end. For a man who revered his Emperor so completely, this was a difficult moment. But Admiral Ugaki had lived by the sword for so long that to take any other attitude was unthinkable for him. He had promised over and over that he would die as he had sent hundreds, thousands, of young men to die, by ramming his airplane into an enemy vessel. He was told that the Emperor would broadcast at noon, and of course he would listen to the words of his God-Emperor. But after that, "I made up my mind to ram enemy vessels at Okinawa, directly leading special attack aircraft, and gave an order to prepare *suisei* planes at this base [Oita] immediately."[15]

The Last Kamikaze

On the morning of August 15, 1945, Admiral Ugaki arose from the sleeping mat in his quarters and put his personal effects neatly together. Then he went to the office to join the officers of his command.

At noon, as Radio Tokyo had been announcing all day, Emperor Hirohito's first broadcast to the Japanese nation was heard. First the national anthem, Kimigayo, was heard; then a high voice that almost no Japanese had ever heard before came on the air. In Oita, far away from the capital, the reception that day was scratchy and ragged, but Admiral Ugaki understood the gist of what the Emperor was saying: The war was lost and he had ended it. The Japanese people must lay down their arms and accept surrender and occupation of their land by the victorious enemy. They must bear the unbearable, but they must go on with life.[1]

When Admiral Ugaki had listened to it all he was numb, filled with chagrin and shame to have been one of those leaders to have brought the nation to such a pass. "I've never been filled with so much trepidation. As one of the officers the throne trusted, I met this sad day. I've never been so ashamed of myself. Alas!"[2]

After the broadcast, several officers came to Ugaki and asked him to reconsider his decision to attack the Americans at Okinawa. The Emperor had called on all his subjects to put down their arms, they reminded him, and to live for a new Japan. He refused to listen to them, saying only that there should be no command difficulties, for his successor as Ten Air Force commander, Admiral Kusaka, was scheduled to arrive that evening. Ugaki had just been appointed to command all the air forces a few hours before the unexpected surrender.[3]

Ugaki's justification for disobeying the direct order of the Emperor to lay down arms and accept the surrender was based on professed ignorance. "We haven't yet received the cease-fire order, so there is no room for me to reconsider. I'm going to follow in the footsteps of those many loyal officers and men who devoted themselves to the country, and I want to live in the noble spirit of the special attack."[4]

In a few words he assessed the recent past:

I've been in this post for six months since I received His Majesty's order. As to the brave, hard-fighting of those forces under my command or my operational command, I need add no more here. As their commander, I'm deeply grateful. I'm also glad to see that our cooperation with the army air forces and also with the naval air forces of Formosa was beyond criticism.

There were various causes for today's tragedy, and I feel that my own responsibility was not light. But more fundamentally it was due to the great difference in national resources between both countries. I hope from the bottom of my heart that not all military men but all the Japanese people will overcome all hardships expected to come in the future, display the traditional spirit of this nation more than ever, do their best to rehabilitate this country, and finally revenge [sic] this defeat in the future. I myself have made up my mind to serve this country even after death takes my body from this earth.

Now at 1600 [4:00 P.M.] my staff officers are waiting for me to drink the farewell cup, so I'm going to end this war diary. . . . This war diary covers from an era preceding the outbreak of war up to date and is divided into fifteen volumes. The things mentioned in various entries contain personal and confidential matters, some of which might be top secret. So I entrust this to the secretary of my class association. This diary must never be placed in enemy hands.[5]

So saying, he put down his writing brush, closed the pages, and handed the last entries to the staff officer who would see that they were included with the rest of his papers and effects at Okayama.

He drank a toast with his staff at Fifth Air Fleet headquarters and then picked up a short samurai sword given to him many months earlier by Admiral Yamamoto. He got into the staff car that came up to take him to the airfield where the planes he had ordered were waiting. The staff accompanied him in a motorcade.

At the airfield he stripped the badges of rank off his cotton uniform. He walked to the flight line where eleven torpedo bombers were warming up. On the line stood twenty-two pilots and aircrewmen, all wearing the headbands of the suicide pilots decorated with the rising sun insignia and words of encouragement for the final mission.

The lieutenant who commanded the unit stood in front of the airmen. Admiral Ugaki told him that he wanted only five planes to go on the mission. The lieutenant said he could not let the admiral go alone, and that all the flight personnel of the unit insisted on going too. Admiral Ugaki then thanked them all for their loyalty, shook hands with each member of his staff, and boarded the lead aircraft. The glass canopy was closed. He waved as the aircraft taxied up to the takeoff line, then the pilot raced the engine and took off. The other planes followed one by one; in ten minutes they were out of sight, heading for Okinawa.[6]

On the way, Admiral Ugaki sent a farewell radio message.

Despite brave fighting by each unit under my command for the past six months, we have failed to destroy the arrogant enemy in order to protect our divine Empire, a failure that should be attributed to my lack of capability. Yet believing that our Empire will last forever and that the special attack spirit of the Ten Air Force will never perish, I am going to proceed to Okinawa, where our men lost their lives like cherry blossoms, and ram into the arrogant American ships, displaying the real spirit of a Japanese warrior.

All units under my command shall keep my will in mind, overcome every conceivable difficulty, rebuild a strong armed force, and make our Empire last forever. The Emperor, banzai![7]

That message was received about five hours after the planes took off from Oita. Then, silence.

At Okinawa that evening it was quiet. The officers and men of the American air bases on Okinawa had finished celebrating the end of the war, but routine duty was still performed. In the harbor lay many warships and many cargo ships; aboard them the officers and quartermasters stood watch.

Late at night the radar picked up blips of a flight of planes coming in, and aboard the ships in harbor the noise of approaching aircraft engines could be heard. But night fighters on routine patrol had been vectored out to meet the incoming planes, and when they were determined not to be American they were attacked. The noise of firing could be heard in the harbor, and one by one in the darkness the aircraft plunged into the sea, not one of them striking any of the Allied vessels. Admiral Ugaki's final flight had ended, as did so many of the kamikaze missions, in a last glorious failure.[8]

Afterword

Admiral Ugaki's diary was preserved and kept by members of his family. In 1952 parts of it were published, but some parts were not, since they referred to very personal matters and the family did not consider these to be a part of the war record that Admiral Ugaki was trying to keep. The diary was translated and annotated by Masataka Chihaya, a postwar journalist and wartime naval officer. A copy of it was given to me in 1987 when I was working on research in Japan for *Yamamoto*, which was published in 1990.

Although Admiral Ugaki warned in his parting entry in the diary that it must "never be placed in enemy hands," ultimately the diary did fall into the hands of the enemy. Gordon W. Prange, who served on the staff of General Douglas MacArthur's occupation forces in Japan, had a copy of the Chihaya translation. His literary heirs further annotated the diary using American records and published it in 1991 with the University of Pittsburgh Press under the title *Fading Victory*. By that time Admiral Ugaki would not have cared, for the Americans, rather than remaining the enemy, had become the friends of Japan.

Notes

INTRODUCTION

1. Ebina, *Saigo no tokuko ki* (*The Last Special Attack Plane*), chap. 1.
2. Ugaki diary, October 16, 1941.
3. Ibid.
4. Ibid.
5. Ibid.
6. Ibid.
7. Inoguchi and Nakajima, *The Divine Wind*, pp. 185-86.
8. Hoyt, *Yamamoto*, chap. 18.
9. Ugaki diary, October 16, 1941.
10. *The Divine Wind*, chap. 16.

CHAPTER 1

1. Hoyt, *Yamamoto*, chap. 19.
2. Hoyt, *Japan's War*, chap. 18.
3. *Yamamoto*, chap. 18.
4. Ugaki diary, October 16, 1941.
5. *Yamamoto*, chap. 18.
6. Ugaki diary, October 24, 1941.
7. Ibid., October 16, 1941.
8. Ibid., October 17, 1941.
9. Ibid., October 18, 1941.
10. Author's observation based on notes for *Yamamoto*.
11. Ugaki diary, October 30, 1941.
12. Ibid., various notations about shore leave in October 1941.

13. *Yamamoto*, pp. 117-18.
14. Ugaki diary, November 2, 1941.
15. Ibid., November 3, 1941. Translation of poem by author.
16. *Yamamoto*, chap. 7.
17. Ugaki diary, November 4, 1941.
18. Ibid.
19. Ibid.
20. Ibid., November 6, 1941.

CHAPTER 2

1. Ugaki diary, November 13, 14, 1941; Hoyt, *Yamamoto*, p. 123.
2. Ugaki diary, November 17, 1941.
3. Ibid., November 19, 1941.
4. Ibid., December 1, 1941.
5. Ibid., December 2, 1941. Translation by author.
6. Ibid. Translation by author.
7. Ibid., December 6, 1941.
8. Ibid.
9. Ito, *The End of the Imperial Japanese Navy*, chap. 1.
10. Ugaki diary, December 7, 1941.

CHAPTER 3

1. Ito, *The End of the Imperial Japanese Navy*, pp. 53-59.
2. Ugaki diary, December 8, 1941.
3. *The End of the Imperial Japanese Navy*, pp. 66, 67.
4. Ibid., pp. 68, 69.
5. Ugaki diary, December 9, 1941.
6. Ibid.; Hoyt, *Yamamoto*, pp. 135, 137.
7. *Yamamoto*, pp. 138, 139; Ugaki diary, December 9, 10, 1941.
8. Ugaki diary, December 10, 1941.
9. Ibid.
10. Ibid., December 10, 11, 1941.

CHAPTER 4

1. Ugaki diary, December 11, 1941.
2. U.S. Pacific Fleet war diary, December 1941 (unpublished).
3. Ugaki diary, December 12, 1941.
4. Hoyt, *Yamamoto*, chap. 21.
5. Ugaki diary, December 15, 1941.
6. Ibid., December 22, 1941.

7. Ibid.

8. Ibid.

9. Ibid., December 23, 1941.

10. Ibid., January 1, 1942.

11. U.S. Pacific Fleet war diary, December 1941.

12. Ugaki diary, January 2, 1942.

13. Author's conclusion based on Japanese and American submarine records.

14. Ugaki diary, January 3, 1942.

15. Ibid.

16. Ibid.

17. Ibid., January 5, 1942.

18. Ibid.

19. Ibid., January 8, 1942.

20. Ibid.

21. *Yamamoto*, pp. 145, 146.

22. Ugaki diary, January 15, 1942.

23. Cincpac war diary, February 1942 (unpublished); Ugaki diary, February 1, 1942.

24. Hoyt, *Japan's War*, p. 216.

CHAPTER 5

1. Ugaki diary, February 1942.

2. Ibid.

3. Ibid., February 11, 1942.

4. Ibid., February 15, 1942.

5. *Asahi Shimbun*, February 1942 (newspaper).

6. Ibid.

7. Ugaki diary, February 19, 1942; Cincpac war diary, February 1942 (unpublished).

8. Tojo diaries, February 1942.

9. Ugaki diary, March 24, 1942.

10. Ibid.

11. Hoyt, *How They Won the War in the Pacific*, pp. 80-90.

12. Hoyt, *Yamamoto*, chap. 23.

13. Ugaki diary, April 1942.

14. *Blue Skies and Blood: The Story of the Battle of the Coral Sea.*

CHAPTER 6

1. Ugaki diary, May 1942.

2. Ibid.

3. Ibid., June 1942; Hoyt, *Defense of the Perimeter*, Midway chapters.
4. Ugaki diary, June 4, 1942.
5. Ibid., June 6, 1942.
6. Ibid., June 10, 1942.
7. Ibid.
8. Ibid.
9. Ibid., June 14, 1942.

CHAPTER 7

1. Ugaki diary, June 15, 1942.
2. Hoyt, *Japan's War*, chap. 28.
3. Ugaki diary, June 16, 1942.
4. Ibid. Translation of poem by author.
5. Ibid., June 1942.
6. Ibid., August 8, 1942.
7. Boei Sen Shi Shitsu, eds., *Nanto Sakusen, Kaigun, I Gadarakanaru* (*Southeast Operations, Navy, Guadalcanal 1*).
8. Ibid.
9. Ibid., chap. 3.
10. Ibid.
11. Ugaki diary, August 10, 1942.
12. Ibid.
13. Ibid., August 12, 1942.
14. Ibid., August 21, 1942.
15. Ibid.
16. Ibid., August 27, 1942.
17. Ibid., September 1942.
18. Ibid.
19. Ibid., September 12, 1942.
20. Ibid.
21. Ibid., September 1942.
22. Ito, *The End of the Imperial Japanese Navy*, chap. 6.
23. Ugaki diary, October 6, 1942.
24. Ibid., October 1942; Boei Sen Shi Shitsu, eds. *Guadalcanal*, chap. 10.
25. Ugaki diary, October 18, 1942.
26. Ibid., October 19, 1942.

CHAPTER 8

1. Ugaki diary, October 23, 1942.
2. Ibid., October 24, 1942.

3. Ibid., October 27, 1942.

4. Ibid., October 1942.

5. Ibid., November 1942; Ito, *The End of the Imperial Japanese Navy*, chap. 5.

6. Ugaki diary, November 21, 1942.

7. Ibid.

8. Ibid., November 25, 1942.

9. Boei Sen Shi Shitsu, eds., *Guadalcanal*, chap. 12.

10. Ugaki diary, November 30, 1942.

11. Ibid.

12. Ibid.

13. Ibid., November-December 1942.

14. *The End of the Imperial Japanese Navy*, chap. 6.

15. Ugaki diary, December 1942.

16. Ibid., December 7, 1942.

17. Ibid.

18. Ibid., December 9, 1942.

19. Ibid.

CHAPTER 9

1. Yamamoto observations by author throughout chapter.

2. Ugaki diary, December 1942.

3. Ibid., December 16, 1942.

4. Ibid., December 23, 1942.

5. Ibid., December 13, 1942.

6. Ibid.

7. Ibid., December 20, 1942.

8. Ibid., December 26, 1942.

9. Ibid., December 29, 1942.

10. Ibid., December 31, 1942.

11. *Chichi ga kataru taiheiyo senso, 1 (Tales My Father Told Me From the Great Pacific War*, vol. 1), pp. 116-20.

12. Author's observation.

13. Ito, *The End of the Imperial Japanese Navy*, p. 83.

14. Ugaki diary, December 31, 1942.

CHAPTER 10

1. Boei Sen Shi Shitsu, eds., *Kaigun Sakusen Nan To Homen, II Gadakanaru (Navy Operations, Southeast Area, Guadalcanal 2)*, Notes on future operations.

2. Hoyt, *The Glory of the Solomons*, chap. 2.

3. Hoyt, *The Jungles of New Guinea*, chap. 5; *The Battle of the Bismarck Sea*.

4. Ugaki diary, April 1, 1943.

5. Ibid., April 2, 1943. Translation of poems by author.

6. Ibid., April 4, 1943.

7. Ibid., April 6, 1943.

8. Ibid., April 7, 1943.

9. Ibid., April 8, 1943.

10. Ibid.

11. Ibid., April 14, 1943.

12. Hoyt, *Yamamoto*, pp. 248-49.

CHAPTER 11

1. Ugaki's reminiscence of the death of Admiral Yamamoto, written in his diary in April 1944 on the anniversary of Yamamoto's death.

2. Ibid.

3. Official report of the death of Admiral Yamamoto in the file of Boei Sen Shi Shitsu (Japanese Defense Department, War History Room).

4. Ugaki's reminiscence.

5. Ibid.

6. Official report.

7. Ibid.

8. U.S. Third Fleet war diary, April 1943 (unpublished).

9. Hoyt, *How They Won the War in the Pacific*, chap. 12.

10. Materials in Nagaoka High School Yamamoto museum, Nagaoka, Japan.

11. Ebina, *Saigo no tokuko ki* (*The Last Special Attack Plane*), pp. 143-44.

12. Fukudome, *Kaigun seikatsu yon ju nen* (*Forty Years in the Navy*), chap. 5, pp. 235ff.

CHAPTER 12

1. Ugaki diary, summary, 1943-44.

2. Morison, *History of United States Naval Operations in World War II*, vol. 8, chap. 9.

3. Ugaki diary, February 1944.

4. *History of the United States Naval Operations in World War II*, vol. 8, pp. 131-35.

5. Ibid.

6. Ibid.

7. Ibid., chap. 9.

8. Hoyt, *To the Marianas*, chap. 8.

9. Hoyt, *McCampbell's Heroes*, chap. 6.

10. Ugaki diary, June 1944.

11. *History of the United States Naval Operations in World War II*, vol. 12, chap. 4.

12. Ugaki diary, July and August 1944.

13. Ibid.

14. Ibid., October 1944.

CHAPTER 13

1. Morison, *History of United States Naval Operations in World War II*, vol. 12, chap. 4.

2. Hoyt, *Battle of Leyte Gulf*, chap. 1.

3. Hoyt, *The Kamikazes*, chap. 1.

4. Ugaki diary, October 1944.

5. Ibid.

6. Ibid., October 21, 1944.

7. Ibid., October 24, 1944; *History of United States Naval Operations in World War II*, vol. 12, chap. 9.

8. Ugaki diary, October 24, 1944.

9. Ibid.

10. *History of United States Naval Operations in World War II*, vol. 12, chap. 10.

11. *The Kamikazes*, chap. 7.

12. Ugaki diary, October 25, 1944.

13. Ibid.

14. *Battle of Leyte Gulf*.

CHAPTER 14

1. Ebina, *Saigo no tokuko ki* (*The Last Special Attack Plane*), pp. 154-86.

2. Ugaki diary, February 2, 1945.

3. *The Last Special Attack Plane*, pp. 177ff.

4. Morison, *History of United States Naval Operations in World War II*, vol. 14, chap. 3.

5. Ugaki diary, February 1945; *History of United States Naval Operations in World War II*, vol. 14, chap. 2.

6. Ugaki diary, February 1945; Inoguchi and Nakajima, *The Divine Wind*, chap. 15.

CHAPTER 15

1. Ugaki diary, February 1945.
2. Ibid.
3. Ibid., March 9, 1945.
4. Hoyt, *The Kamikazes*, chap. 19.
5. Ugaki diary, March 1945.
6. Ibid., March 10, 1945.
7. Ibid.
8. Ibid., March 11, 1945.
9. Ibid.
10. Ibid.
11. Morison, *History of United States Naval Operations in World War II*, vol. 14.

CHAPTER 16

1. Ugaki diary, February 1945.
2. Hoyt, *The Kamikazes*, chap. 20; Hoyt, *Tojo's War*, chap. 18.
3. Ugaki diary, March 1945.
4. Ibid.; Morison, *History of United States Naval Operations in World War II*, vol. 14, pp. 130ff.
5. Ugaki diary, March 1945.
6. Ibid., March 18, 19, 1945; *History of United States Naval Operations in World War II*, vol. 14, chap. 7.
7. Ibid.
8. Ugaki diary, February 1945 and March 21, 1945.
9. Ibid.
10. *History of United States Naval Operations in World War II*, vol. 14, p. 100.

CHAPTER 17

1. Ugaki diary, March 25, 1945.
2. Morison, *History of United States Naval Operations in World War II*, vol. 14, pp. 117ff.
3. Ugaki diary, April 1945.
4. Ibid.
5. Ibid., April 1945.
6. Ibid., April 12, 1945.
7. Ibid., April 13, 1945.
8. Ibid., April 17, 1945.

9. Hoyt, *The Airmen*, pp. 383ff.; Ugaki diary, May 1945.

10. Ugaki diary, May 6, 1945.

11. Ibid., May 11, 1945.

12. Ibid., May 1945.

13. Ibid., May 30, 1945.

14. Ibid., June 3, 1945.

CHAPTER 18

1. Ugaki diary, June 1945.

2. Ibid.

3. Ibid.

4. Ibid., June 12, 1945.

5. Ibid., June 18, 1945.

6. Morison, *History of United States Naval Operations in World War II*, vol. 14, pp. 309ff.

7. Ugaki diary, July 1945.

8. Ibid., August 1, 1945.

9. Ibid., August 1945.

10. Ibid., August 9, 1945.

11. Ibid.

12. Ibid.

13. Ibid., May 1945.

14. *History of United States Naval Operations in World War II*, vol. 14, pp. 330ff.

15. Ugaki diary, August 14, 1945.

CHAPTER 19

1. Ugaki diary, August 15, 1945.

2. Ibid.

3. Ibid.

4. Ibid.

5. Ibid.

6. Ibid.; Inoguchi and Nakajima, *The Divine Wind*, pp. 185, 186.

7. Ibid.

8. Letter to author from Victor Hubbard, freighter deck officer whose ship was in Naha harbor on the night of August 15, 1945.

Selected Bibliography

Boei Sen Shi Shitsu, eds. *Sen shi sho so*. 101 vols. (Japan Self-Defense Force War History Room, ed., *War History Series*). Specifically the volumes on Guadalcanal, New Guinea naval operations, Hawaii operations, Midway, the Marianas, and Leyte Gulf, and the two volumes on Defense of the Homeland. Tokyo: Cho un shin mon sha, 1950-1970.

Chihaya, Masataka, trans. Donald M. Goldstein and Katherine A. Dillon, eds. *Fading Victory: The Diary of Admiral Matome Ugaki, 1941-45*. Pittsburgh: University of Pittsburgh Press, 1991.

Dyer, George C. *The Amphibians Came to Conquer* (A biography of Admiral Richmond Kelly Turner), 2 vols. Washington, D.C.: U.S. Government Printing Office, undated.

Ebina, Kenjo. *Saigo no tokuko ki* (*The Last Special Attack Plane*) (A biography of Matome Ugaki). Tokyo: To sho sui han sha, 1975.

Fukudome, Shigeru. *Forty Years in the Navy*. Tokyo: Ji ji to shin sha, 1971.

Hoyt, Edwin P. *How They Won the War in the Pacific*. New York: Weybright and Talley, 1969.

_____. *Battle of Leyte Gulf*. New York: David McKay, 1971.

_____. *To the Marianas*. New York: Van Nostrand Reinhold, 1978.

_____. *The Glory of the Solomons*. New York: Stein and Day, 1979.

_____. *McCampbell's Heroes*. New York: Van Nostrand Reinhold, 1979.

_____. *The Kamikazes*. New York: Arbor House, 1983.

_____. *Japan's War*. New York: McGraw-Hill, 1986.

_____. *The Airmen*. New York: McGraw-Hill, 1989.

_____. *The Jungles of New Guinea*. New York: Avon Books, 1989.

_____. *Yamamoto*. New York: McGraw-Hill, 1990.

_____. *Defense of the Perimeter*. Avon, 1992.

_____. *Hirohito*. New York: Praeger, 1992.

Inoguchi, Rikihei, and Tadashi Nakajima, with Roger Pineau. *The Divine Wind*. New York: Bantam Books, 1958.

Ito, Masanori, with Roger Pineau. *The End of the Imperial Japanese Navy*. New York: W. W. Norton, 1956.

Morison, Samuel Eliot. *History of United States Naval Operations in World War II*. 14 vols. Boston: Atlantic Monthly Press, 1950-1970.

Ugaki, Matome. *Sen So Roku (Seaweed of War)*. Tokyo: Nippon Shuppan Kyodo Kabushiki Kaisha, 1952.

UNPUBLISHED MANUSCRIPTS

Hoyt, Edwin P. *Tojo's War*. Scheduled for publication in 1992 by Madison Publishers.

Ugaki, Matome. *Seaweed of War*. I used the Japanese version published in Tokyo. I also used a copy of the English translation made by Masataka Chihaya, which was given to me by the translator several years ago when I was preparing *Yamamoto*. Since that time an annotated version has been published by the University of Pittsburgh Press; I also used that version.

U.S. Strategic Bombing Survey (Pacific). Washington, D.C.: U.S. Government Printing Office, 1947.

Index

About the Author

EDWIN P. HOYT is a popular military historian who has written widely on the Pacific War, Japan, and China. He is the author of *Japan's War*, *The Militarists*, and *The Rise of the Chinese Republic*. His most recent book with Praeger is *Hirohito: The Emperor and the Man* (1992).